PIVOT POINT

Reshaping Your Business When It Matters Most

Sheri Jacobs, FASAE, CAE

Emily Thomas, Editorial Advisor

asae®
association
management
press

WASHINGTON, DC

Pivot Point: Reshaping Your Business When It Matters Most

The author has worked diligently to ensure that all information in this book is accurate as of the time of publication and consistent with standards of good practice in the general management community. As research and practice advance, however, standards may change. For this reason it is recommended that readers evaluate the applicability of any recommendations in light of particular situations and changing standards.

ASAE: The Center for Association Leadership
1575 I Street, NW
Washington, DC 20005-1103
Phone: (202) 626-2723; (888) 950-2723 outside metropolitan Washington, DC area
Fax: (202) 220-6439
Email: books@asaecenter.org

We connect great ideas and great people to inspire leadership and achievement in the association community.

Keith C. Skillman, CAE, Vice President, Publications, ASAE: The Center for Association Leadership
Baron Williams, CAE, Director of Book Publishing, ASAE: The Center for Association Leadership

Cover design by Kundia Wood, ASAE: The Center for Association Leadership
Text design by Troy Scott Parker, Cimarron Design

This book is available at a special discount when ordered in bulk quantities. For information, contact the ASAE Member Service Center at (202) 371-0940. A complete catalog of titles is available on the ASAE website at www.asaecenter.org.

ISBN-13: 978-0-88034-397-8

Printed in the United States of America.

10 9 8 7 6 5 4 3 2 1

To my family, Jillian, Jodie, Allan, and Debbie—
I am eternally grateful for your love and support. You inspire me.

To Greg Fine—my friend and work husband—
how lucky are we to go down this path together.

To Jon—fiercely and forever.

Contents

Acknowledgements

To the following individuals, listed in alphabetical order, I extend my sincere appreciation for sharing their time, stories, and support.

Pierre Désy, MPH, CAE
Abe Eshkenazi, CSCP, CPA, FASAE, CAE
Halee Fischer-Wright, MD, MMM, FAAP, FACMPE
David Gammel, FASAE, CAE
Chris Gloede
JP Guilbault
Velma Hart, FASAE, CAE
Chris McEntee, MHA, FASAE
Jeff Morgan, FASAE, CAE
Susan Neely, CAE
Jamie Notter
Peter O'Neil, FASAE, CAE
Sue Reimbold, MA
Dawn Sweeney, FASAE
Don Welsh
Catherine Wemette, CAE
Scott Wiley, FASAE, CAE

I also wish to acknowledge the Avenue M Group team for all their contributions: Matthew Cavers, Nick Fernandes, Keith Holzmueller, Roya Meshulam, and Trevor Schlusemann.

Finally, I am grateful to Emily Thomas, the editorial advisor on this book. I could not have written this book without her enthusiastic support and contributions.

Introduction

When I first proposed the idea of this book, I expected at the end of writing it to have a set of three or four business model templates to propose for associations. But after interviewing association c-suite executives and thought leaders and learning how they transformed organizations to address a changing environment, I realized their stories were not just about designing the best business models for their associations. Rather, the stories were about cultivating nimble organizations that could continually adapt their value propositions *and* business models to address changes in the needs, attitudes, and behaviors of the communities they serve. In short, the story became about how to pivot. It's perhaps fitting that I had to pivot the focus of this book from what I planned on sharing to the story I observed once I had all the pieces in front of me.

Why Business Models?

The meeting began like so many others. A collection of senior staff representing a variety of departments assembled to discuss their organization's strategic goals and the challenges they were facing in achieving them. Past efforts to move the needle and help the association reverse a trend of declining membership and engagement had little to no effect. Every few years, they conducted a membership needs assessment to identify needs, motivations, challenges, and trends. But when faced with implementing major changes based on the research findings and trends within the marketplace, the staff faced a few roadblocks. The bylaws dictated who could be a member of the organization, thereby limiting the marketplace to the same declining group of individuals. And funds were limited for investing in new ideas and new technology to spur engagement to increase retention rates.

The organization convened a membership task force to evaluate and discuss a list of options, including opening up membership to new audiences and creating new opportunities for younger members to engage. Discussions were held regarding creating an organizational membership program, but little movement had been made in this direction. Everyone in the room agreed that it was time to make some changes, but no one could agree on the right approach—and this, along with a fear of failure, paralyzed the organization. And so, year after year, they continued to focus their efforts on improving their marketing and communication while making minor adjustments to the value proposition.

The scenario I just described occurs with such frequency that if I exchanged my notes from one kick-off meeting with another, it would be difficult to discern any differences.

Nonprofit is a tax status, not a business strategy. It's a statement I find myself repeating when I speak with volunteer leaders and association executives. And while many of the individuals I speak with *know* this to be true, it can be difficult to operate as such when they work in an environment that is highly risk adverse and steeped in tradition. Volunteer leaders may have a desire to change, but when push comes to shove, they don't want to change. There is a perception by many that staying the course is less risky than expanding investments of time and money into new audiences and benefits.

At its core, a business model is how an organization makes money. To provide the content and education members need or to advocate on behalf of the profession, an association needs revenue. A frequently used axiom in the healthcare community is "no money, no mission." I see a kind of tug-of-war in the mentality of many associations, regardless of industry: the association is intended to represent and support members so that they can succeed in their field, but the association needs members' financial support to do so.

An association's business model is the collection of its revenue streams, including membership dues. If a main source of revenue starts to dry up or if changing trends on the horizon suggest a source may not be around for much longer, an association must be prepared to pivot and change its business model. More importantly, if your organization waits until it begins to *see* a decline in membership, participation, or revenue, it is more difficult to shift priorities.

For decades, the holy grail of membership has been an organization's ability to provide access to research and information, advocacy, and an exclusive community of peers. Discounts on education and publications and access to affinity programs are also frequently bundled together in exchange for a dues payment based on different demographics. Many organizations promote their unique qualities by highlighting the depth, rigor, and thoroughness of their offerings. But times have changed, and the attributes that were highly valued in the past now take a backseat to accessibility, flexibility, and affordability. Members may value the high quality and thoroughness of an organization's guidelines, standards, and informational resources, but if they are not digital, condensed, and easy to access and use, those members will turn to another resource. In other words, members and potential customers are prioritizing a frictionless transaction or experience. Although this book does not advocate abandoning the core strengths traditional organizations bring to the table, I do believe it's essential for associations to understand and respond to the market forces driving the decisions to join and engage with associations and use their resources.

I often see associations make small changes in an attempt to fix big challenges. They adjust the price of membership when the core issue is a lack of value to members. They redesign their websites but don't improve the accessibility and usability of content, which is often the cause of members' frustrations. When associations see a stagnation or decline in membership dues, they talk about membership models and pricing—I've built my company on helping associations create new membership models and pricing structures—but without value, people won't give their money or their time.

As attitudes and values shift from ownership to access and flexibility, members will be drawn to organizations that provide real solutions that address their challenges and meet their needs. And while a passion to advance a cause or support a chosen industry still drives some individuals and companies to join an association, most organizations will need to find new ways to appeal to those who seek a transactional relationship or simply wish to find a resource that quickly resolves an issue.

While many organizations view the changes in behavior and attitudes I've described as threats, I believe these changes instead create opportunities for organizations to expand their reach and advance their missions. But this will require organizations to be nimbler in how they operate, make decisions, and deliver value. For some, that might mean a shift from a revenue model based on membership dues to alternative sources of value and revenue. Others may need to focus on creating new experiences, new methods for sharing information, and new ways to provide value in a rapidly changing environment. Associations need to think beyond membership models and consider how membership fits within a more comprehensive business model. And to make the shift, they need to examine their volunteer governance structures and work cultures to ensure they can support the changes needed to remain relevant.

The Perfect Business Model ... Doesn't Exist

What I've learned from conducting interviews with the executives and thought leaders in this book is that there is not one ideal business model out there, just like there isn't one ideal membership model or pricing strategy that works for every association. And while you can identify effective practices and insights by evaluating the models being used by other associations, the key to helping your organization thrive in the future is not replicating another organization's business model or strategy. Embracing change, especially when success is uncertain and the risk of failure is fairly high, is extremely difficult for most associations, their professional staff, and their volunteer leadership.

How you make money, how you deliver value, who you serve, and what value you give—all of these can change. The secret is to cultivate the ability to pivot to achieve your mission. Drawing from interviews with association c-suite executives and thought leaders, this book explores the pivot point—the how, why, and when an association should pivot to meet changes in the community it serves and the world overall.

This Book: What to Expect

While there is no ideal business model that works for all associations, there are common characteristics that associations need in order to have the ability to pivot. Creating a culture that can pivot when needed is hard. It requires associations to be more responsive and nimble and to embrace change—even when there is a risk of failure.

Chapter 1 illustrates the landscape we are all facing, regardless of industry: the continual changes in technology, the workforce, consumption habits, and other wide-ranging factors influencing our professional and personal lives. Chapter 2 outlines the essential characteristics of a nimble association that can pivot to meet changes in the environment. In Chapter 3, I explain why organizational culture is crucial to implementing change. Chapter 4 dives deeper into how to build a value proposition—and how to be prepared to change it. Chapter 5 covers how to use research to guide change, including selecting a new membership model. And finally, Chapter 6 explores the sharing economy and some of the companies building business models around access instead of ownership. Throughout the book, I include interviews I conducted in early 2018 with c-suite executives and other thought leaders in the association community. At the end, I share my observations on the common qualities exhibited by these association executives and thought leaders.

CHAPTER 1

●

A Changing Landscape

When I was looking to join a gym many years ago, my priorities included its proximity to my home, the hours of operation, and the selection of cardio classes. If the club offered an upscale locker room where I could get ready for work, that was a bonus. Price was a consideration, but it was secondary to the other factors. The membership structure was virtually the same for every health club in my area at the time. The clubs required a 12-month commitment and an initiation fee with some clubs offering the options of using the facility during nonprime hours for a discounted monthly fee. Many of these traditional health clubs are still in business, and their value propositions meet the needs of those who use them on a regular basis. However, scores of individuals, such as myself, eagerly abandoned their memberships when boutique studios opened. For me, it was Orangetheory Fitness while many of my friends joined Club Pilates and CorePower Yoga. All three studios offered pay-as-you-go or short-term membership plans. I could join for three months, six months, or pay monthly and cancel anytime. Plus, with locations across the United States, it offered more options for me to work out when I was traveling. When I first learned of Orangetheory Fitness, I signed up for one of the Orange Premier unlimited sessions per month memberships. Over time, I've switched between this level and the Elite membership which includes eight sessions per month. I've moved up and down the membership levels based on how frequently I used the gym. Both options offered a month-to-month membership, and at no time was I required to sign a lengthy contract. Had the studio maintained a traditional membership model, including a 12-month commitment and a cancellation penalty, I would have most likely just been an occasional customer and looked for a more flexible option elsewhere.

The goal of most associations is to capture the attention (and financial support) of everyone who wishes to access their resources, including those who have resisted joining because they don't find enough value in the current bundle of benefits—very similar to health clubs. As someone who has been involved in the association community since 1996, I have observed several trends in the ways people want to engage with associations. As the example above illustrates, one of those trends is cord-cutting. Many people are moving away from options that require a long-term commitment to a one-size-fits-all set of benefits. In a January 2017 white paper my company, Avenue M Group, created, "5 Trends Your Association Shouldn't Ignore," we identify several other trends that affect how people want to engage with services and consume information. For one, many consumers expect personalized, responsive customer service and will stop doing business with a company that doesn't guarantee a good customer experience. Another trend is the transition to a sharing economy; new business models are emerging (think Uber and Airbnb) to take advantage of a shift from ownership to convenient access. These trends and others—explored in more depth later in this book—signal a change in how people, especially members of younger generations, want to interact with and become involved in professional associations.

As we have learned over the last 20 years, associations can no longer dictate the terms of engagement. In many cases, you must build a model that includes alternative paths to engagement. As these trends grow—and I don't expect them to revert anytime soon—it is essential for organizations to develop a strategy to expand their reach and grow their customer base.

Cause-Based Versus Member-Based

Are you a cause-based organization, or is your primary focus to serve the needs of your members? This is one of the first questions I ask an organization considering a new membership or business model. Organizations centered around a cause frequently have mission statements that focus on advancement of a profession or of a broader enterprise such as science, medicine, the arts, finance, law, or the well-being of patients or humanity. By comparison, organizations focused on individual members or their employers will include in their mission or vision statement a focus on helping their members succeed or achieve their goals. When you read your organization's mission and vision statements, do you see the word *member?*

While many professional associations consider both the profession and the professional, most have a primary focus in one or the other, and a key indicator is the association name itself. If the formal name mentions the professional rather than the profession (e.g., pediatrician rather than pediatrics), this typically indicates its strategic priorities center on meeting the professional or business development needs of the professional—that is, the member. As a member-centric organization, success is often measured by percentages: the percentage increase in new members, the percentage of current members who renew, the percentage of members who engage or participate in programs, and so forth. Volunteer leaders often review the numbers on a quarterly basis, and the organization uses this information to demonstrate its influence within the industry or profession. While nearly all individual membership organizations allocate resources to improving society through their efforts to inform, educate, certify, and advocate, an organization's mission, vision, and core values often reflect its primary strategic focus. In the case of member-oriented associations, that focus is the advancement of members.

For cause-based organizations, membership may be only one of their product lines, a way to build long-term relationships with individuals and encourage them to contribute their thought leadership, time, and resources as volunteers and supporters of the organization. Success is more often measured by the depth and breadth of the association's reach, and the use of resources by customers as well as members (in other words, engagement) is a key performance metric. As such, while membership numbers are measured, the business model that cause-based organizations often use focuses more on the delivery of programs, products, and services.

Whether you are with a cause-based organization or member-centric association, you are probably facing significant challenges due to a shifting landscape. It is important to identify the opportunities in these shifts. And for many associations, that means a new business model to capitalize on these opportunities. As leaders evaluate new business models for their organizations, they need to frequently remind themselves who they are serving, assess the amount of change they are able to manage, and contemplate the level of risk they're willing to take. And they need to ask themselves if the current board and staff culture will embrace the change. Sometimes an organization will not experience the positive results of change until after an initial dip in revenue, membership, or engagement. The alternative to change, though, is stagnation, and staying the course despite a changing environment may eventually become a slide into irrelevancy.

Consider the lifespan of the companies currently listed on the S&P 500, which according to Investopedia.com, is the preferred index for U.S. stocks and is perceived as more representative of the market because it uses a market cap methodology, giving a higher weight to larger companies. According to a report from Innosight, a growth strategy consulting firm, approximately 50 percent of the S&P 500 companies could be replaced over the next 10 years,[1] a dramatic change from a few decades ago.[2] Years ago, the list of companies on the S&P 500 included Kodak, Radio Shack, and Circuit City. All these companies were leaders in industries that still exist and thrive today. These companies and others that went bankrupt and dropped off the S&P 500 failed to respond quickly as market forces and advances in technology changed consumer behavior. Today, if an organization does not continually invest in new technology or change how it delivers value, the repercussions will be more immediate, and the organization may not have enough time to respond.

While no one has a crystal ball, it's easy to see why this prediction may materialize. A quick glance around my house tells the story behind the change in consumer preferences and behavior. It also illustrates how I became a new customer to many companies that didn't exist five years prior.

Because of the time constraints from both running a company and raising a daughter, I wanted to make certain aspects of managing a home easier. I also wanted more control and flexibility. Rather than pay for a landline, for example, I realized my smart phone was a better choice for staying in touch with friends and family. I also didn't need to sign a long-term contract with the cable company. Instead, I could access my favorite television shows and movies through one of the digital streaming companies, such as Hulu, Sling, Netflix, or Amazon. I discovered several new apps and devices that gave me more control over actions, such as controlling the temperature in my house, turning on the lights, and activating the security system. At least once a week, I order household items online and have them shipped to my home or office. Even the process of ordering from Amazon has changed. With Alexa, I can ask the device to order or reorder items while I am making dinner or doing other tasks around the house.

Many of the companies that develop and sell the products I use today are considered disruptors, creators of a new or more efficient way of doing something. Disruption occurs when an organization captures the attention of an underserved market, which in many cases consists of those who are not currently customers or members.[3] In the association community, this may include students or colleagues of members—in other words, groups who are not the primary audience served by the organization. When a for-profit company enters the association space and competes head-to-head with the traditional association, it may disrupt the way business gets done or information is delivered if it offers a more effective way to achieve similar results. The entry of for-profit companies into continuing education delivery comes to mind as an example of this.

Not every innovation is a disruption. Ultimately, if a disruptor is to succeed, it usually incorporates an improvement in how an existing product or service is delivered using an affordable, digital, and accessible solution. If it solves a problem or improves a situation, it may disrupt the traditional way of doing business—even if the goal remains the same.

Uber and Airbnb are common examples given of disruptors because they successfully entered established industries with new business models that addressed common problems. The goal may still be a ride to the airport or a place to stay on vacation, but the way to accomplish the goal has changed.

Identifying opportunities for disruption is not easy. To build a new business model, organizations can't simply ask their members, "What could we offer you that would provide more value or help solve a problem?" If you had asked me five years ago if there was anything I needed or wanted that didn't exist, I could not have come up with an answer. Instead, if you had asked me to chronicle my life for a week or asked about the most frustrating or no longer useful items in my home, I may have identified a few of the items I have replaced with new products and services that were not available a decade ago. It's the job of the organization to pinpoint common pain points among members and propose potential solutions.

When companies with an established business model decide to reinvent themselves, many wisely begin by focusing on a core offering or strength they can leverage. For many associations, their core offerings include continuing education, research and information, and career advancement or business development opportunities. Other organizations advocate on behalf of the profession, a service that benefits everyone in the industry regardless of their membership status. While the delivery channels may have changed, each of the core benefits still provides an essential service because it helps keep members updated, compliant, competitive, and informed. Unfortunately, this may not be enough to form a strong connection between the organization and the member. Benefits must address pain points or challenges in a way that is accessible, affordable, and relevant.

Consider the physician who needs to look up specific information during a patient consultation to make a treatment decision. It's inefficient and time consuming to open a web browser on his or her phone or tablet, go to a general search engine, and sift through results for a solution. The information needs to be a few clicks away so that he or she can quickly determine a treatment and provide the best advice. When looking for a resource that will help the physician achieve this specific goal—or what Clayton Christensen refers to in his theory of *Jobs to be Done* as "to make progress"[4]—he or she is most likely to use a resource that is accessible and reliable during the point of use. Convenience and ease of use become more important than brand reputation and a rigorous review process. That is because while the latter—brand reputation and a rigorous review process—may be important characteristics of the organization or its product, the former—convenience and ease of use—are directly about the needs of the customer. Keeping the customer or member at the center of decisions may seem like an easy task for associations, especially individual membership organizations, but too often even associations lose track of what's most important to the people they serve.

Using Value to Guide Transformation

With the shift in many healthcare specialties to a more care-team focused model, many healthcare associations must address the question of who they serve if they wish to achieve their missions. Should they expand their purview to the entire healthcare team or maintain their focus on the primary audience they have historically served? Expanding your audience requires more than establishing a new membership category; without value for those new audience segments, a new membership category will have minimal impact on association growth. To truly establish a new membership model and business plan overall that will expand your audience, you need to put value at the center of any pivot to a new direction—and that's exactly what CHEST, formerly only known as the American College of Chest Physicians, did.

When Sue Reimbold, MA, arrived at CHEST, a new strategic plan had recently been approved that would put the association on a path better aligned with the changing landscape in healthcare and health systems. CHEST saw an opportunity to be a global leader in chest medicine, education, and research, but it would require some significant changes to who it served and what benefits it delivered. As part of this strategic plan, the association wanted to grow the organization while also growing revenue. One of the strategies was to transform its membership model. As Reimbold recalled, "The strategy was to evolve the membership model to increase community and engagement within the chest community." Rather than setting the goal as a growth in membership numbers, CHEST aimed to grow engagement and increase usage of its programs, products, and services.

The volunteer leaders and senior staff at CHEST knew the importance of using the question of value to guide the transformation. Questions such as, what is the value proposition for each audience—an established practitioner versus someone just kicking off their career? What is the value for a non-physician who might find our resources helpful but not traditional membership? Putting value at the center of the discussion laid the foundation for designing a business plan and membership model that responded to the changes in healthcare.

To expand the CHEST audience, a committee of volunteer leaders and staff examined the existing portfolio of programs, products, and services and evaluated how they could provide value to members of the entire chest medicine team. "We wanted to increase access," said Reimbold. "Who else can benefit from the content? They don't all join as members, but by thinking about who we serve and what we offer, we had to rethink the business we are in and how we achieve our goals." One area where CHEST expanded its reach was in the content of the Live Learning Courses at the CHEST Innovation, Simulation, and Training Center. Reimbold stated, "These courses, traditionally viewed as courses for doctors, had to be repositioned as offering content that was available to— and relevant to—other members of the team, and we encouraged doctors to share promotion of the courses with their colleagues across nursing, respiratory care, physician assistants, as well as doctors who fell outside of pulmonary/critical care/sleep medicine but who could benefit from the content." CHEST also repositioned the annual board review courses to be open to the whole healthcare team and expanded education offerings to meet the continuing education credit needs of nurses, respiratory therapists, and so forth.

In addition to repositioning the content of its offerings, CHEST looked at the delivery channels. Recognizing that not all physicians can take time off from work and family obligations to attend live courses, the association created an on-demand board review product. There was concern that offering an online alternative would lead to lower attendance at the live courses. While this is a common and valid concern among many associations, Reimbold noted the important takeaway to keep in mind— establishing the online alternative can create a new revenue stream from those who would be unable to attend the live event. This was part of a larger strategy CHEST enacted, which was looking at the larger trends in how people consume information. "It's about making things available for people in how they use them. We aren't in the events business. We don't think about what products and events we sell; we now think about content and deliver it in a way that people use it," said Reimbold.

In addition to recognizing a trend in the way people access information, the staff observed changes in how people chose to engage and stay updated. "People want to self-select on how they want to engage and what they put their money to. We started looking at the exchange for value because that was going on in other sectors in our members' lives. You pay for more benefits. Do you go with regular Amazon or Amazon Prime? Do you pay for the VIP experience at a concert? We looked at those examples and focused on building a model with democratizing tiers that allows our members to choose." When crafting that model, it was important to look outside the healthcare space. Reimbold recalled, "It opened up a new dialogue. We didn't just ask, 'What are our competitors doing?' We looked at who was increasing engagement. We looked at universities, museums, and nonmedical associations. For me, it was about looking outside the box and building a business model oriented around building community." CHEST needed a model that would support its expanding reach. As a result of looking outside the healthcare association community, CHEST was able to implement a model that enabled members to choose how to engage with the organization based on their needs.

One piece of advice Reimbold offered is not to rush change. "With a business model change this big, it takes a while for a board to understand. They were accustomed to pricing changes or name changes or tweaks, but this type of model change takes time. We went to every board meeting, giving them time to digest and retooling the infrastructure and processes when necessary." The change took two years. The first year was spent acquiring the necessary buy-in from the board. And the second year included developing new communication and operating procedures and finalizing the plan and budget.

Often, leading such a substantial change also means making some unpopular decisions along the way and halting the implementation of certain projects mid-scope. For example, when Reimbold joined the team, the organization was investing in a new association management software system (AMS). Reimbold recognized that building out requirements based on how the old system worked would cause problems down the line, so she paused the update to requirements to reflect the evolving membership model in the new AMS. "Being new to the staff and calling a time out wasn't popular because they had put time into it. The team building out AMS requirements of our membership model had to change gears. There was sunk cost already in the update to a new AMS, and you can't get that back." Reimbold stated that she's glad she called that time out to ensure the system they created could support the new model.

As part of the shift in audience and value, Reimbold championed a rebranding that would encapsulate the association's change in value and audience. "I was brought on as the senior VP of marketing to refresh the brand. As a new leader for marketing with this experience from health-care systems, I took advantage of rebranding to emphasize CHEST instead of American College of Chest Physicians. The old name worked with the old model. We emphasized CHEST because that reflected our new model."

Though they didn't set out to increase the number of members, by reframing how they approached membership, those numbers did grow. "In 2013, we had just under 18,000 members. We didn't set a metric, but now in 2018 we have 20,000-plus members because we thought about membership differently as well. For our event, we encouraged people to bring their team. We focused on creating content and messages for the entire team. For the first time in the organization's history, we had four straight years of meeting attendance over 4,000."

Reimbold reflected on the crucial elements that led to the success of the membership model change: "I think when you change your membership model, it should be a directive of the board and part of the strategic plan." Reimbold added that the success was because of "the combination of strategic plan and board support, having resources committed to it, and a consultant to help us think outside the box and look at trends outside our sphere. Looking outside the box for the value equation and how to price it—that was the core piece that helped us evolve."

Lessons Learned From CHEST

1. To ensure the board fully embraces any changes to the organization and its membership, engage them as active participants early in the process. This goes beyond giving them status updates or interviewing them as key stakeholders. Set aside time at a board meeting or retreat to discuss the challenges and opportunities based on the current climate.

2. Don't be afraid to pause or sunset programs when necessary. It's never too late to pivot or pull the plug on an investment if it no longer aligns with the direction or needs of the organization and the new business model. Think about the long-term consequences rather than the short-term costs.

3. Be prepared for minor successes and failures and make course corrections, if needed. Change doesn't happen overnight. Advise the volunteer leadership that it may take time to realize the positive results of changes to the organization.

The Death of Toys 'R' Us and Borders

Amazon and Walmart did not cause the demise of Toys 'R' Us or Borders. These companies died because they took their eyes off the customer. For Toys 'R' Us, problems intensified after private equity firms did a leveraged buyout and saddled the company with debt. After seven decades of selling toys, Toys 'R' Us informed its employees and customers it would close or sell its U.S. stores in 2018. Although shoppers were familiar with the brand and many had a tradition of shopping at the retail store, online and offline competitors offered a better shopping experience, better prices, and a larger inventory. Being encumbered with significant debt, Toys 'R' Us could not make the necessary investments to update its physical stores or online platforms. By the time Amazon started selling toys and games online, often at lower prices and with two-day delivery, Toys 'R' Us had to focus its resources on "paying off that massive debt load rather than staying competitive," wrote Chris Isidore on CNN Money.[5]

As for Borders, it operated more than 1,200 bookstores and employed more than 30,000 people at its peak in the 1990s.[6] Although Amazon is frequently blamed for the death of the brick-and-mortar bookstore, the most likely culprits are missteps from Borders, including ignoring the needs of the customer, dismissing opportunities to grow its online platform, and failing to track and adjust to changing habits related to the consumption of books, music, and video.

As opportunities to access "what we want, when we want it" increase, traditional ways of doing business will no longer meet the needs of all consumers. What drives change, in any industry, is the need for a more efficient and cost-effective transaction—a frictionless experience. Satisfaction occurs when expectations are met. What I've seen and experienced time and again is that loyalty to a brand, organization, or product takes a backseat when innovation and new technology offer a better solution at a lower price. And consumers will not return to the old way of doing business.

Focus on the Future, Not on the Past

Although 2017 marked its 90th anniversary, the Club Management Association of America (formerly Club Managers Association of America) (CMAA) is more interested in focusing on its future than its past. Not unlike many other associations, CMAA created programs and products to support the needs of an audience that had remained unchanged for decades. From country, golf, and city clubs to faculty, yacht, and military clubs, CMAA's members run the organizations that employ 345,000 individuals and serve more than 1.8 million members. And while the private club community has evolved more rapidly in recent times to meet the changing needs of individuals and families, the organization realized its value proposition had not progressed with the changes occurring in the profession.

Years ago, the club management profession typically attracted individuals who grew up near a club and had either some experience working at a club or the desire to move into a management position. CMAA's value proposition was structured around serving the education and training needs of individuals who held either a high school diploma or a college degree. It was fairly uncommon to see someone enter the profession with a graduate degree or as a transition from another field. As such, CMAA's professional development program, the Business Management Institute, offered an opportunity to achieve various levels of competencies and knowledge to successfully manage a club. Over time, however, the pathway to club management changed. As Jeff Morgan, FASAE, CAE, the chief executive officer of CMAA, observed, professionals in club management are more transient, and they are entering the position from nontraditional roles. "As professionals moved into management positions after spending time as a golf instructor in the PGA or working in a luxury hotel chain, it was clear that their needs were different from those who had advanced from the traditional path of coming from food and beverage positions. The demographics had changed, but the association was still offering the same programs, content, and training programs geared for an audience that was quickly shrinking." The changes in the demographics and professional pathways in the industry required a change in the value CMAA delivered.

When Morgan was hired as CMAA's CEO in 2014, the board made the decision to seek the expertise of someone from the association community rather than from the club community. They knew it was time to shake things up and begin making changes if the organization was to thrive in the future. And shake things up is what Morgan did.

One of the first items on his agenda was to review CMAA's entire portfolio and ask how each offering served its members. The result of this exercise helped CMAA expand its offerings and create a resource center for club staff beyond the general manager. In the previous model, only two or three individuals on the club staff used CMAA's benefits, yet many of the resources could benefit a variety of staff roles, from senior management to seasonal workers.

Morgan recognized that if he created new programs to better meet the needs of the workforce, it would require redirecting resources and possibly sunsetting or updating some programs. It would also require identifying and addressing the unresolved pain points his members were facing today and not the more common problems of years past. Morgan stated, "One thing we are doing right now is addressing the specific issues that keep club managers up at night. How do I keep my members and their families safe? Who am I competing with in my local community? How can I create a high-end and personal experience? The needs of country clubs can be vastly different from the needs of city clubs. Some may have retirees, some may serve business professionals, and some may offer children's activities." Morgan knew they needed to know the industry and the range of unique challenges their professionals face for CMAA to provide solutions.

To stay on top of trends and be more nimble and responsive to needs, Morgan spends more than a third of his time on the road visiting clubs and learning what innovations and experiences they are creating. He sees this as an important role for CMAA—to share new ideas and new approaches so that members may learn from one another and be successful. However, Morgan is not alone in this pursuit. Today, more than 250 individuals (up from 75 before Morgan joined CMAA) serve on task forces in areas where they have a strong interest. "We are the association experts; they are the industry experts. We want to put skin in the game for them," Morgan explained.

CMAA is member-owned, and Morgan considers his members to be owner operators. He taps into his community of members to help identify what's new, what's next, and where the industry is going, including what value may no longer be relevant. The old business model treated every member the same, regardless of their geographic location, club type, or the members they served. Morgan does not believe a one-size-fits-all business model is sustainable. Different types of members have different needs because they are addressing different issues and challenges.

When considering a new benefit, Morgan and his staff now ask if and how it will solve a member problem. When Morgan arrived at CMAA, the culture was top-down. Decisions were made by the senior executive, and the staff was bound to execute on them. This did not create an environment that could adapt to changes in the marketplace and pivot their approach to delivering benefits as trends emerged. Today, CMAA is team-oriented and participatory. It's all about serving their members. Under Morgan's leadership, CMAA recognizes the value millennials and an overall diversity of thought bring to enhancing the organization's value proposition. "We now have parity of voice. We create cross-cultural teams to tackle issues, and we consider ourselves entrepreneurs." The responsibility for the organization's success is shared among all members of the staff and leadership.

While CMAA has made important strides to remodel the club of clubs, more changes are on the horizon, including a name change. As of July 2018, CMAA became the Club Management Association of America, changing *Managers* to *Management*. While this may appear minor, it signals a broader focus on expanding the organization's value proposition beyond those currently serving in a manager position. CMAA is investing in new benefits and services for professionals in a variety of positions at clubs. The board approved a CMAA Fellows program that will act as a hall of fame, recognizing outstanding club management professionals. CMAA is also adding new elective sports and recreation courses that focus on non-golf activities as well as children/youth activities and others. Another way CMAA is expanding its reach beyond club managers is through a program focused on both managers and their board members. In 2018, it will hold four governance leadership summits. Rather than looking at the summits as profitable revenue streams, Morgan sees them as a more effective way to build awareness of CMAA among audiences who have a hand in deciding if clubs should join, continue membership, and engage with the association.

To ensure CMAA continues to be nimble and responsive to the changing needs of its members and the profession, Morgan frequently asks himself, what can I do to serve my members very quickly and bring new ideas to the market quickly? His priority is to get the ideas out to play as fast as possible. "Some will grow, and some will die, and some will evolve. Instead of creating the perfect car, I want to get a frame and wheels out there and hear how members are using it and refine it once I see how they use it." He continued, "Associations can be slow because they look at budgets and projects. At CMAA, we try things, even knowing some will be terrible ideas. This gives my members and staff a lot of energy because there isn't a long waiting period to get things out, so they are encouraged to do more. This process feeds on itself."

Morgan admits that change gives his board members anxiety, but they understand he won't take the association too far down a major change pathway without examining new ideas, the risks, and the possible rewards. For Morgan and his staff, it's a never-ending process of assessment, evaluation, trial, and error with the goal of coming up with breakthrough ideas that will resonate with today's club management professionals.

Lessons Learned From CMAA

1. Change requires risk and uncertainty. The value proposition that served your organization well in the past—established its name and built a loyal member base—is often not the one that is needed to ensure relevancy in the future. Change also requires courage and leadership, from the board to the CEO. By pivoting the decision-making process from a top-down approach to a more equal playing field, your organization will be better positioned to adapt and respond to changes in the market. If you wait until the demand is at its peak, you are likely to have missed an opportunity to lead rather than follow. Not every idea will succeed, but you will establish a reputation for being a leader, an organization that will take some risks so that its members may learn.

   a. Do your current membership model and portfolio of benefits still meet the needs of your market?

   b. Does your organization only launch new programs and products that it is highly certain will succeed?

   c. Is your board ready to take on new initiatives that have not been tested?

   d. Does your organization set aside a percentage of its budget to test new ideas, even if they may not succeed?

2. Invest in bringing a range of perspectives to the table. Diversity and inclusion are essential if you wish to be responsive to the changing needs of your market. Market segments are becoming more fragmented

and diverse. The one-size-fits-all approach no longer serves the needs of many members.

    a. How well do you know the different audience segments within your member and customer base?

    b. Do your volunteer leaders serve in positions that reflect the industry today or the one that existed when the organization was formed?

    c. Are members of different audience segments and career stages represented on key volunteer committees and councils? Do they have a voice in the development and investment in new programs or products?

3. Make it a priority to stay current with changing career paths within the profession. Some individuals are entering the profession as a second career, sometimes in their 30s or 40s. Others are transitioning through less conventional methods.

    a. Is there a new path to career advancement within your industry?

    b. Does career advancement require a different set of skills, knowledge, and experience than what was previously required? Do your members and prospects have access to the tools they need to get ahead?

    c. Are your certification programs and educational content aligned with the changes taking place within your industry or profession?

    d. If there is a global opportunity to expand your reach, are you positioned to leverage your strengths and enter new markets? If not, have you considered partnering with or acquiring another organization that is already providing these needed services?

●

CHAPTER 2

Five Essential Characteristics

Every organization, regardless of size, geographic scope, or industry, will face a situation that requires changing how it delivers value to its members, customers, and other key stakeholders. For some organizations, this may be the emergence of new competitors, advances in technology, or a changing workforce. For others, changing consumer behavior or changes in the regulatory environment necessitate the organization to adapt. The only thing you can be certain of is that change is constant. Understanding the key characteristics that help an organization become more nimble and responsive to market changes is essential if you want your organization to remain relevant. In other words, the true path to relevancy is creating a culture that can pivot when needed.

The pivot point will vary by organization, but five essential characteristics foster an organization's ability to pivot. Many of these five characteristics reflect the changing ways people in the United States consume products, obtain information, and share experiences. The five essential characteristics are

1. Access(ibility)
2. Flexibility
3. Affordability
4. Diversity and Inclusion

5. Trust

These five characteristics go beyond just implementing programs, products, and services that are accessible, flexible, affordable, etc. They should be part of the mindset of association leaders as they manage change and cultivate a nimble association.

The first characteristic, access(ibility), encompasses two concepts that, though connected, have important, nuanced differences: access *to* something and accessibility *of* something. The former refers to a key dimension of many association offerings: access to education, access to information, access to community, etc. We are witnessing the beginning of a trend toward access instead of ownership. People may want access to something but may not feel a need to own it. They also may not consider membership as part of their professional identity. And more and more people are foregoing access if access requires being saddled with a one-size-fits-all commitment, as in the example of gym membership at the beginning of Chapter 1. As consumers' interactions with for-profit companies change, their expectations of their professional associations also shift. Anyone who has been working in or around associations for more than a decade has probably heard or even stated the following: "membership is the lifeblood of an association." There's truth in the statement, but acknowledging the necessity of members to an associa-tion's existence does not require an end game of converting everyone to members. To expand your reach, there should be options for individuals or companies to access the association or its offerings as customers or subscribers because revenue is *also* necessary for an association's existence. Treating membership as the only valuable connection may be holding many associations back from achieving their mission—and yes, even holding them back from best serving their members. Associations will need to consider types of access beyond just membership.

The other concept is accessibility, which is more about the delivery of the programs, products, and services to which associations provide access. As associations consider the different levels of access to benefits, they will also need to consider how to align the delivery of those benefits with how people use them. Your organization may provide access to content, but is that content in a format and on a platform that is accessible and therefore valuable? Many medical organizations, for example, provide access to in-depth, trustworthy guidelines, but if those guidelines are not accessible at the point of care, members and prospects may look elsewhere. While we are witnessing a shift in the desire for access without commitment, we have been witnessing for years the changes in *how* people access and use an organization's products and services. A nimble organization needs to be able to monitor and respond to trends in both access and accessibility.

The next characteristic, flexibility, is entwined with access and accessibility. Associations recognize flexibility is the key to growth, like offering many options for accessing and using the benefits of membership or providing multiple payment options. They must be flexible in starting, adjusting, and sunsetting offerings to keep up with the changing needs of members and customers. Associations, however, also need to consider flexibility in who can affiliate and how they can affiliate.

The third characteristic is affordability. Having an affordability mindset is not about the lowest price possible but instead considers external factors (e.g., compensation, student debt, job security) affecting members' evaluation of price relative to value. For example, who's paying for the dues or the product—if the employer pays the bill, will they see the value in what your association is offering? As another example, many associations offer membership to secondary or tertiary audiences at a price significantly lower than that of full members, but recruitment and retention remain low for those groups despite the price. In many cases, though, the price by itself is not the issue; it's the price relative to value. Having an affordability mindset is not about setting the lowest possible price but about always keeping an eye on whether members will see the value as *worth* the price.

Diversity and inclusion comprise the fourth characteristic. As I will discuss in more detail later in this chapter, diversity and inclusion should be understood as a business strategy for integrating a range of backgrounds and perspectives into decision making; it's not a checklist based on demographics. A common example in associations is the early career professional. Although this individual may be invited to serve on a committee or the board, his or her insights may not be integrated into the strategic direction of the association.

The final characteristic is foundational to achieving an association capable of pivoting: Trust. Volunteer leadership must trust that the staff will implement on the decisions they make, and staff must trust the volunteer leadership to make decisions based on the best interests of the association as a whole. Without trust between the board and staff, an otherwise nimble association with the other four characteristics will not be able to implement and manage change.

These five essential characteristics represent the qualities associations need to adapt to and implement changes:

- Access(ibility) beyond membership
- Flexibility beyond one-size-fits-all affiliation
- Affordability beyond just price
- Diversity and inclusion beyond tokenism
- Trust as the foundation to implement the other four characteristics

At the end of this book, I provide a guide inspired by these five essential characteristics to help associations evaluate their readiness to pivot.

Open Nights and Weekends

Earlier this year, I came home from work one Friday afternoon and heard a loud humming noise seeming to originate in my basement. As I descended the staircase, I discovered nearly a foot of water surrounding my water heater and spilling into other areas of my basement. Unable to find the valve to stop the flow of water, I grabbed a pair of boots and a bucket and began to bail. After posting a few photos on Facebook and receiving advice from friends who had been in similar situations, I found the valve, stopped the water from leaking, and mopped the floor, but the damage had been done. The carpet was ruined, and my plans for the weekend just changed. I had to contact my insurance company by Saturday evening and file a claim. I wanted to get a remediation company out as soon as possible and get my basement back to a usable space.

In years past, I would have waited until after eight or nine on Monday morning to make the call. Because Mondays are usually the busiest day of the week for service companies that are closed over the weekend, it could have taken longer to get through to an agent, file a claim, and begin the cleanup and replacement work. These days the experience is completely different. Over the weekend, I used my insurance company's mobile app to file a claim. Within the same day, it arranged for a remediation expert to visit my home and make sure my walls and floors were dry. I was able to place an order for new carpeting within a day or two, and a check arrived to reimburse me for my expenses before my credit card bill with those expenses arrived.

When disaster strikes, you want a solution that is effective and efficient and works within your timeframe—in other words, a solution that is designed to be *accessible* and efficient because it fits into your life. You begin to not only value these benefits when offered but also expect them. Your interest in buying from organizations that do not offer accessible, effective solutions wanes. Unless the benefits offered are unique or require a high level of personal interaction, you expect a baseline of accessibility that gives you more control over timing and method of contact.

In the association community, we are witnessing a shift to this baseline of accessibility in members' expectations of interactions as well. Consider the experience members or customers encounter when they visit your organization's website seeking a solution to a specific problem. Do you make it easy to find a solution, such as a webinar, article, resource, or tool? Is it easy to download a resource, register for an event, or obtain the information they need when they need it? Or are they overwhelmed with information, products, programs, and resources? Access is more than dumping as much information as possible on a webpage—it requires guidance to a solution for a specific problem. If your organization offers comprehensive and detailed information but lacks personal guidance, customer reviews, or recommendations for other related products, visitors are unlikely to complete transactions or return the next time they have questions.

Today's members and customers are savvy online consumers. They become repeat customers of websites that make it easy to find what they need and provide peer reviews and online answers when they have questions. Does your organization ask questions to understand the potential buyer's level of knowledge and experience? Does it provide any guidance regarding what courses and publications are most relevant based on what they hope to learn and the format that is most useful for them? Do you offer reviews and testimonials from others who have used or read the resource? Although your organization may provide a detailed description of a program or product, if it lacks the ability to provide guidance based on the personal and individual needs of the customer or member, it's unlikely that person will engage. (I expand on this more in the section titled "It's Not Customer Service … It's Customer Experience" later in this chapter.)

Consider the early career professionals within your industry. It's the first week on the job, and they are asked to perform tasks they didn't learn in school. Their supervisors may not have the soft skills or time to train them, and they are left to search for some resource, tool, or online educational course to explain how to complete the tasks they've been assigned. They conduct a search on their mobile devices and come across your organization's website. Although the information and education you provide is reliable and detailed and even though your brand name is recognizable, if the website isn't user-friendly and if the content isn't accessible (like optimized for a mobile device), they may leave your organization and never return.

Many for-profit organizations that are competing with associations use artificial intelligence to map different customer journeys through their websites to provide real-time guidance and advice. Using digital tools and data intelligence to improve customer service is becoming the standard for any organization wishing to build or expand its customer base. When an organization offers guidance and information tailored to a customer's immediate needs, it is more likely to develop a stronger connection and encourage repeat purchases.

Accessible, Flexible Solutions

When it comes to addressing the daily challenges in my professional and personal life, I seek solutions that are easy to access and will save me time. If I run out of toner for my office printer, I will purchase a replacement cartridge on Amazon rather than drive to an office supply store because purchasing it online is frictionless, and I can get back to work quickly. My credit card information and shipping address are in the system, and it's easy to find the items I need. For busy professionals, saving time and having confidence in the transaction are two factors that drive behavior. In fact, access and efficiency are more important than brand loyalty for many of today's transactions. And while this isn't the case for every transaction, occasionally I will switch to a new brand or provider if it meets my immediate needs. The few exceptions to this behavior are reserved for products and experiences that cannot be obtained elsewhere. As I write this paragraph, however, it's difficult to think of many situations where this still exists. Although I may build a relationship based on trust and satisfaction with a service provider, such as a pharmacist, hair stylist, or eye doctor, if they are unable to provide what I need when I need it, I will turn somewhere else and may not return.

One of the many benefits of web-based services is the ability to find, view, research, and purchase goods and services when it fits into your schedule. Hours of operation are no longer a barrier to completing a transaction. Think back to your last vacation. If you are like most people, the days leading up to your departure were probably jammed with appointments, meetings, and last-minute tasks so that you could enjoy a brief respite from the chaos of your daily life. Working late to finish that last assignment might mean missing Barnes & Noble's open hours to get a new beach read. Of course, with it and many other booksellers online, the task of searching for, buying, and accessing a new e-book to read is one task that can be completed within minutes. Flexibility beyond hours of operation is not limited to online shopping, banking, or making reservations for a flight or hotel. Your members' searches for solutions won't just happen during your association's office hours. Associations should expect an increase in competition as other companies explore new ways to deliver solutions that are flexible enough to accommodate members' needs.

A Digital Doctor Visit

Within a matter of minutes, I knew I had made the right choice. It was a few days before I was to leave for a vacation in Scotland, and I came down with a bad cold. My throat was sore, and my head was congested. A persistent cough kept me up at night, and I thought I might have a low-grade fever. I knew I needed to see a doctor soon or face a miserable nine-hour flight from Chicago to Edinburgh, including a two-hour layover in London. I didn't have time to schedule a visit to the doctor. A friend recommended I check out one of the telemedicine apps and schedule an appointment that fit into my schedule. After a brief search, I found one that offered 24/7 availability for appointments, provided a licensed health-care provider in my state, and accepted a variety of payment options or insurance. The fee was comparable to my co-pay, and I could schedule and have the appointment in the comfort of my home around my schedule. I was sold.

Scheduling an appointment and filling out my profile took less than five minutes. The app was easy to use to search for a provider and upload my health history. I scheduled my appointment for 7:30 p.m., and my doctor arrived on time. She asked a few questions and within minutes of the call suggested a course of action to minimize my symptoms. She also sent my prescription to the pharmacy around the corner from my house. Although telemedicine may not be the solution to resolve all health issues, the emergence of this alternative approach to dealing with a common and easily addressed problem will forever change how I view my relationship with healthcare providers.

Looking over the pain points of seeing a doctor for a common and minor condition, it is clear a more efficient and flexible way to meet some healthcare needs exists. Consider the steps you take every time you visit a doctor: 1) Calling the doctor's office and waiting on hold while they serve patients who are waiting in line at the counter. 2) Adjusting your schedule to fit into the time slots available, if any exist. 3) Taking time off work or away from other obligations to visit the doctor. 4) Sitting in the waiting room with other sick patients, waiting for an appointment that is rarely on time. 5) Checking out and submitting a co-pay for the visit.

Although the practice of providing patients with remote diagnosis and treatment plans has existed for decades, the emergence and availability of the internet, videoconferencing, smart phones, and mobile apps have significantly increased its usage and made it more affordable in some cases. It is important to note that the pivot in the delivery of medical care occurred before the service was widely used by patients. In hindsight, any organization or company could have predicted the popularity of this type of service if it had identified the pain points to receiving medical care and tracked the use of mobile phones for different activities. And while it is easy to be critical of organizations that ignore trends, exploring the reasons why this occurs is important. It will identify the weaknesses in your organization and help you manage and even embrace change.

Organizations have a choice when it comes to following a business plan to achieve their missions. They can build a culture that easily adapts to changes in behavior, or they can maintain a business strategy built on a legacy system. One choice involves taking a risk while the other stays the course, making only minor changes or adjustments. And although every macro-indicator—including a decline in the number of new members, meeting attendance, and purchases of programs and products—points to an overall decline in interest in professional membership organizations, many organizations still believe staying the course is the less risky path.

Organizations thriving in today's economy can easily justify staying the course. Why shift your focus if your current value proposition meets the needs of your audience? In fact, your organization may be experiencing an increase in demand for its products, or registrations to your conference may be at an all-time high. Most executives and volunteer leaders would look at the performance of its primary revenue streams and feel confident the best course of action is to maintain or increase investments in current activities. Yet with the rapid advancements in technology, organizations that are not agile and focused on delivering their benefits in the most efficient manner will realize that making little to no change is its own risk.

How do you know the right path for your organization? When should you pivot and take a new approach, create a new value proposition, or shift your focus from serving one segment of your market to other segments? It begins by assessing your culture, changes within your market, and the external factors impacting decisions to join and engage. By collecting, aggregating, and analyzing data from a variety of sources, your organization will be better prepared to identify changes before they impact your organization. By identifying and understanding the trends in the profession better than their members, organizations can invest in benefits (i.e., programs, products, and services) members are most likely to need to thrive in the profession.

Changing What Isn't Broken

> "Make no little plans; they have no magic to stir men's blood and probably themselves will not be realized. Make big plans; aim high in hope and work."
> —Daniel Hudson Burnham[1]

The National Restaurant Association is the largest food service trade association in the world, supporting more than 500,000 restaurant businesses. In partnership with its state restaurant associations, the national association's mission is to empower all restaurant owners and operators to achieve more than they thought possible. One of its roles is to represent and advocate for food service industry interests, taking on financial and regulatory obstacles before they hit its members' bottom lines. The Restaurant Association also offers tools and systems for member organizations of all sizes, helping them achieve better operating results. Because of its large, active membership base, the organization is able to provide unique networking, education, and research resources.

Since joining the organization as CEO in 2007, Dawn Sweeney, FASAE, has focused her efforts on a wide range of policy issues, while strengthening programs, products, and services that promote the industry and help individual operators and large multiunit companies succeed. The restaurant industry is one of the primary engines that drives the local, state, and national economies. "The impact of our industry's vitality extends far beyond our own restaurants' walls. Restaurant sales generate tax dollars for local communities, and our huge number of employees—14.7 million—translates into healthy contributions to state and federal tax revenues," said Sweeney.

Similar to other organizations profiled in this book, National Restaurant Association leadership sees a direct link between staying on top of emerging trends and saving members time, money, and headaches by helping them take on what matters most for their success and growth. Sweeney stated, "We strive to move our industry forward by finding answers to the tough questions, distilling complex information into practical knowledge, and helping our members navigate the issues facing small businesses. And that makes us the go-to resource for smart, relevant intelligence that helps our members run their businesses better." During her time as CEO, Sweeney has realigned the association's priorities and structure to strengthen its core operations, including consolidating its foundation around a mission to develop a strong workforce and build the next generation of industry leaders. The National Restaurant Association Educational Foundation's major goal is to educate students on the restaurant business through the ProStart program, running in high schools nationwide, and to provide educational scholarships. These efforts support the Foundation's mission focused on strengthening the industry and building the workforce for the future. By monitoring trends in its industry, the Restaurant Association was able to create programs and products that gave members access to the information they needed to stay updated.

The Restaurant Association also supports its membership by showcasing members and industry trends, distributing information, and providing sessions and education on emerging trends. One of its key channels for achieving this is its annual convention, the largest restaurant and hospitality tradeshow in the United States. Each May, more than 65,000 food service professionals, vendors, and others come to Chicago to attend the National Restaurant Show. While other tradeshows have experienced a decline in attendance, sponsorships, exhibits, and advertising, across the past 10 years, the Restaurant Show has grown both in size, revenue, and influence. Under Sweeney's direction, the Restaurant Show offers a unique opportunity to explore the latest trends and developments in menus, equipment, technology, and operations. In addition to the learning that happens from demonstrations and talks on the tradeshow floor, the Restaurant Show includes programs on how to increase revenue and on sustainability within the industry.

Even though the 2018 Restaurant Show attracted the largest number of attendees in its 99-year history, Sweeney and her team have plans to reinvent the Restaurant Show for 2019, timed to coincide with its 100th anniversary. Although many organizations plan activities and events to celebrate a major anniversary, it's even more important to demonstrate how the organization has evolved to remain relevant. By introducing new ideas and experiences that will impress, excite, and engage attendees, Sweeney believes participants will continue to find value in the event. "We are of the opinion that the best time to reinvent something is when it is at its peak of success. Therefore, we are doing this with our Restaurant Show. Internally, we are calling this effort SHOW 2.0, with an eye toward driving even greater industry success (that is, restaurant and hospitality career and business) through the platform of our annual Show." Sweeney added, "Our overall association and foundation multi-year strategy is grounded in building the industry's influence, engagement, and image, and our Show is key to achieving all three of these." Although many organizations would shy away from changing something that isn't broken and potentially risking a decline in attendance and revenue, Sweeney asserts this is the time to make changes to ensure the Restaurant Show continues to provide an experience focused on where the industry is going, not solely where it's been.

As part of this reinvention of its event, the Restaurant Association is focused on protecting its assets while also transforming and growing its impact. "We want to accelerate our digital transformation to create more of a live media experience and to allow our attendees to create more personalized, curated experiences. Much of our efforts will be tied to a greatly enhanced data strategy, greater on-floor educational content, and more on-floor event areas and activations."

To ensure the organization continues to evolve, Sweeney has a five-year board strategy and a two- to three-year internal plan. Sweeney stated, "I don't want a 24-hour period to go by where we haven't advanced the ball. We have to feel that we moved the ball down the field. We do a lot of forecasting for our budgets. We have multiple options we are pursuing. Some don't work out, and some do." Because of the unpredictability of what works and what doesn't, the Restaurant Association's leadership has built flexibility into its model.

Sweeney added that one of her mantras is to make big plans. "That's my secret. No matter where we are on anything—I say double it. We've done that many times in several places. Since I joined the National Restaurant Association, we've more than doubled our revenue, from $50 to $120 million. Now we are planning to double it again. We will be at $200 million pretty soon and then $300 million." The large organization avoids becoming stagnant by frequently shifting how it addresses members' concerns and provides solutions. The easiest route to take is one that requires little change, but staying the course is unlikely to help an organization double or triple its revenue.

Lessons Learned From the National Restaurant Association

1. Build a culture of trust and introspection. Volunteer leaders are more likely to support new ventures that have a plan based on data and a strategy for course correction if key metrics are not met during the trial and error phase. Without trust between staff and volunteers, national and state, and the organization and its members, an organization cannot make the changes needed to pivot.

2. Set big goals. For many organizations, this is something they *say* but don't *do.* Often, they set goals based on what they think they can achieve in a short amount of time. But when pivoting to meet a changing market, it is essential to set big goals and link those goals back to the changes you need to make. Explaining the purpose behind the goal will make it easier to justify investing in a strategy to achieve big goals. Big goals will encourage volunteer leaders and staff to think differently and develop new approaches to engaging your audience. Modest goals will not require an organization to evolve its approach to expanding its reach or creating exceptional experiences.

3. When you reach the big goals you've set, change your strategy or try something new—make a pivot. The National Restaurant Association

plans to use the momentum it's built in the last decade to change its strategy and try something new. Making changes to a business model that is achieving its goals may seem risky and unnecessary. It will undoubtedly leave some volunteer leaders and staff questioning your sanity. To overcome their objections, present a list of new ideas, products, and companies that displaced the traditional ones that stayed the course after achieving success.

4. Strengthen your core operations to enhance your value proposition, increase engagement, and increase revenue. This can be accomplished by aligning staff, resources, and products with the needs of the markets you serve. Set key performance metrics, including participation and profit goals, for major product lines. If a program or product is profitable but reaches a very small audience, it may put a strain on resources that could be allocated to another program.

5. Don't place all bets on one horse. The likelihood of failure is much higher when only one idea is tried. Instead, create an idea bank based on trends affecting your members and industry. Preferences, experiences, behaviors, and attitudes change. If you don't change your portfolio of benefits, you risk losing current and prospective members to competitors. Budget and plan for beta testing numerous ideas or concepts. Not every new idea should require considerable resources during beta testing. For example, you could change the venue and approach of an existing networking event, explore a new subscription model to measure interest in your content, or partner with a company to deliver a new benefit to your members.

Setting a Big Goal—Then Doubling It

Years ago, while I was serving in a senior membership position at a regional association, the board set a goal of achieving a 17 percent increase in membership after 10 years of no growth. At first, my colleagues asked how I could possibly achieve that. And some even wondered if I had been set up for failure. Given this goal, I recognized that I had more room to experiment and didn't need to rely on only the safe, "tried and true" methods. I, therefore, changed my strategy and took bigger risks, testing new tactics and new approaches to growing membership. By the end of the year, we doubled the goal and increased membership by 34 percent. In *The Art of Membership: How to Attract, Retain and Cement Member Loyalty,* I detail some of the strategies and tactics we used to successfully grow membership.

An important aspect of accessibility is user-friendliness, and associations are finding that many members and customers prioritize ease of use over any other quality. In the healthcare community, many medical associations compete against products such as UpToDate, an evidence-based, physician-authored clinical decision support resource designed to help clinicians make the right point-of-care decisions. According to UpToDate's website, it is used by more than 1.3 million clinicians in 187 countries. The product offers evidence-based topics that are accessible on a mobile device, making it available at the point of care, and clinicians can subscribe for a low monthly rate and cancel anytime. Its marketing promotes it as reliable, user-friendly, and affordable while offering flexible payment and commitment options.

Just as some factors, like user-friendliness, are essential to the success of a new product, failures can occur because the product is launched too soon or too late, the technology cannot support the product, or audience behavior has not yet adapted to new methods for consuming information or education. In addition, some products fail because the organization attempted to overcome bad design or functionality with a promotional campaign. Clever marketing is not a long-term solution for a faulty product.

When Google unveiled its new product Google Glass in 2012, it received rave reviews and widespread promotion. The product appeared in *Vogue* magazine and on the fashion runway. It was showcased on many of the morning and evening news shows, *The Colbert Report,* and in YouTube videos. Oprah, Beyoncé, and other celebrities tried it out and shared their experiences with their fans. *Time Magazine* identified Glass as one of the "Best Inventions of the Year 2012." Joshua Topolsky raved about Glass in his review on *The Verge:* "The more I used Glass the more it made sense to me; the more I wanted it. ... After a few hours with Glass, I've decided that the question is no longer 'if,' but 'when?'"[2] Today, Glass is considered a major product failure, alongside New Coke, Sony Betamax, and Apple Newton.

In a *New York Times* article, Nick Bilton examined Google Glass' failure to launch by exploring the dissent within Google and the individuals assigned to the project.[3] According to Bilton, while some members of the team believed Glass should be worn as a "fashionable device" and accessory, others believed it should be worn on a more limited basis for specific functions. A public testing of the product failed to provide the feedback or generate the interest Google was seeking. However, the biggest challenges were due to the product itself; many critics cited product bugs, a short battery life, and privacy concerns.

Ultimately, wearable technology became extremely popular and widely used three years later. If you look around your organization or office, you will likely see some of your colleagues wearing a Fitbit or Apple Watch. When wearable technology succeeds, it does so because it is user-friendly, accurate, and reliable. In the case of Fitbit, it provides a community or connection to others who are tracking their steps. Successful wearable technology provides an easy-to-use, unobtrusive solution to an issue or challenge.

The challenge most organizations face, including those with deep pockets like Google, is creating a structure that will embrace trial and error and make course corrections when plans fail. It is equally important to ensure past failures do not prevent an organization from trying new ideas, launching new products, and expanding their reach into new audiences. Incubating a new idea requires a structure that tests and learns quickly. In other words, organizations that make a commitment to testing new concepts while using data to make decisions are more likely to achieve growth and success in a rapidly changing environment. They must be able to pivot quickly and learn from mistakes or product failures.

A great business model requires a commitment to tracking trends, collecting data, and experimenting with new ideas. To enhance an organization's knowledge of the profession and the behavioral trends impacting

To help organizations ensure they are not left behind as attitudes and behaviors change, *ASAE ForesightWorks User's Guide* encourages the use of a customized version of the common framework STEEP (social, technological, economic, environmental, and political) to systematically scan for evidence of change.[4] Although such a tool is useful when it is customized to an organization's industry, the *User's Guide* also recommends scaling back efforts to two or three action briefs from *ASAE ForesightWorks* to achieve useful results.

BUSINESS
Media
Business Practices
Consumer Life
Work
Marketing
Events
Publishing & IP

POLITICS
Global Politics
Government
Activism
Political Shifts
Lobbying & Advocacy

TECHNOLOGY AND SCIENCE
Environment
Non-IT Technology
Healthcare
IT & Automation
Science
Energy
Data Analysis
Social Media

Current Domains

Governance
Events & Networking
Education & Training
Operations
Outreach
Money
Member Engagement

SOCIETY
Information & Knowledge
Education
Demography
Social Life
Values
Accountability
Training & Development

ECONOMY
Globalization
Emerging Markets
Economic Conditions
Market Conditions

decisions, it's important to take a longer view and consider the drivers of change that will have long-term repercussions on the organization. This requires research, analysis, foresight, and leadership buy-in and support. According to Marsha L. Rhea, CAE, in the ASAE *ForesightWorks User's Guide,* "Associations can use foresight to support four important purposes:

1. To support strategic planning and strategy development.

2. To inform anticipatory learning.

3. To conduct risk analysis.

4. To inspire innovation and business development."[5]

To successfully navigate fast-changing landscapes, the executives interviewed for this book were proactive in their decision making rather than waiting for changes in the market to hamper participation or revenue. For many, this required adopting an attitude of *fail fast and learn.* But they didn't venture into new spaces without paying attention to the trends and drivers of change. They collected research and made data-based decisions, but they were not paralyzed by indecision nor did they wait until they had complete confidence that a new initiative would be successful. They knew that waiting until all the evidence was in might mean waiting until it was too late to act.

It's Not Customer Service ... It's Customer Experience

> **"... People remember the customer service a lot longer than they remember the price."**
> — Lauren Freedman, president, E-tailing Group[6]

> **"We take most of the money that we could have spent on paid advertising and instead put it back into the customer experience. Then we let the customers be our marketing."**
> — Tony Hsieh, CEO, Zappos[7]

Given the choice, I'd rather not call a customer service center and speak to a live person to resolve an issue or find an answer. And I'm not alone. According to a survey conducted on behalf of Helpshift (a customer-service platform), 55 percent of American consumers want chatbots—that is, computer programs using artificial intelligence to conduct a conversation—involved in customer care; that number jumps to 65 percent among millennials.[8] This desire for choice of customer service channels isn't new. A 2013 report from Aberdeen indicates that companies with "weak omnichannel strategies" retain on average only around one third of their customers, while companies with the "strongest omnichannel customer engagement strategies" retain 89 percent on average.[9] How can associations create an omnichannel strategy for customer service? They must invest in and expand opportunities to ensure customers and members have options when they need assistance.

From the simplest of tasks, such as paying back a friend for lunch or checking in for an upcoming flight, the two most important factors when making the decision to use a product or service is often accessibility and convenience. Often, my first choice for connecting with a company is through a chatbot. Even when you call an 800 number for a larger company, you will most likely speak with a chatbot before you are directed to a person. When thoughtfully created and updated, chatbots provide an experience that feels like you are interacting with a live person but give you the convenience of finding answers or solutions when and where you need them. A bonus to the consumer is shorter wait times.

Many questions asked of customer or member experience desks at associations can be easily answered through an automated system. Think about the needs of early career professionals within your industry or profession. By examining the purchasing behavior of individuals based on the year they passed an exam or completed an undergraduate or graduate program, your organization should be able to create a list of recommended courses they should take as they advance in the profession. This information could be used to help guide early career professionals in making decisions regarding what courses they should register for or products they should buy. From selecting a course of study to advance in one's career to locating mobile-friendly tools and resources, associations have the opportunity to increase engagement and demonstrate their relevancy in an increasingly competitive environment.

The fact that your organization offers the highest quality information or education may not be a strong enough selling point to recruit and engage new members or to persuade potential customers to choose your products over those of competitors. Instead, members and customers are looking for fast answers that allow them to solve their issues and move on quickly to the next task. When they need assistance and must contact your organization, the ease of this experience, combined with a satisfactory resolution, will increase the likelihood they will return and tell others about the experience.

Remember that flooded basement I mentioned earlier? I was able to file a claim with my insurance company, submit receipts for the cleanup, and order the replacement carpet all online. The response time was immediate, and knowing the issue was resolved quickly, I felt empowered. Within 24 hours, a cleaning crew was at my house, and I was already selecting a new carpet for the room. By midday on Monday, I was the proud owner of a new, more efficient water heater. The only time I spoke with a live person was when the insurance company called to follow up and ensure I was satisfied with the process.

Building a reputation for providing an exceptional customer experience is essential to an organization's long-term growth. Today, that requires delivering the experience in a way that is favored by its customers, members, and users. Whether you manage a luxury hotel or a regional or state organization, some members and customers are likely to desire a high level of personal touch. But you will also need to provide options for those who seek easy access to answers and solutions via their mobile devices.

A week before I left for a vacation in San Francisco and Napa Valley, I received an email from the hotel where I planned to stay, asking if they could do anything to help me plan for my upcoming visit. The email included links to its website, the email address for the concierge who would be on the property during my stay, and a suggestion to download the mobile app for additional convenience. The day before I arrived, the mobile app sent a text message (I opted in to receive the communication) inviting me to check in and select from a variety of options to personalize my stay. This particular hotel is well known for its high level of personal touch, and it provides numerous options for improving the experience of guests. In years past, if you needed additional towels or pillows or wanted to order room service, you needed to call the hotel operator or guest services. Today, I can use the app to order room service, to request items I may have left at home, or to contact the concierge to help make dinner plans.

Understanding the preferred method of communication and the behavior patterns of your customers improves the overall experience and increases satisfaction. In light of how customers consume or use products and interact with companies, it is no surprise they are turning away from organizations that have not updated their delivery methods for their products and services. Ilan Mochari, a senior writer for *Inc.,* wrote, "A company cannot endure in the long term without reinventing itself. Which means leaders have to be vigilant for what the [Innosight] report calls 'fault lines'—the weakening foundations in your business model, or the shifting needs of your customer base."[10] Expectations for receiving the same level of service will undoubtedly carry over from the consumer world to the association community. If there is a widening gap between how your organization delivers its benefits and provides customer service and how they are delivered in the consumer world, you may see a decrease in membership and engagement.

As preferences for digital, accessible, and affordable products move individuals to engage with organizations that meet their needs, associations need to adapt their current portfolio at a more rapid pace. In *ASAE ForesightWorks User's Guide,* the author predicts traditional educational models will find increased competition from online education and alternative credentialing systems that offer a free or highly discounted offering. As an example, *ForesightWorks* cites the State of the MOOC 2016 report from Online Course Report, which records the growth in massive open online courses from 160,000 participants at one university in 2011 to 35 million participants at 570 universities in 2016.[11] As a solution, the *User's Guide* identifies microlearning and other direct-to-learner digital education as a growing opportunity for associations. The actions recommended include helping students navigate their education options, partnering with new education providers, and moving quickly when universities move slowly to update curricula.

The recommendations included in this book may seem like a tall order if you work at or run a small association with limited resources. Unfortunately, the expectations of your current members and prospects are equally as high. See "Size Doesn't Matter" for a look at how one smaller organization is planning ahead to meet those expectations.

Size Doesn't Matter

Fifty years ago, when a group of likeminded fellows of the American College of Obstetricians and Gynecologists gathered, the seeds were planted for creating an organization focused exclusively on issues related to gynecologic cancers. Three years after the formation of the Society of Gynecologic Oncologists, it convened its first annual meeting. Since that time, the organization has not shied away from change, including making the pivot in 2011 to its current name, the Society of Gynecologic Oncology (SGO) to reflect a move to serve the entire cancer team (and not just oncologists). Today, SGO's vision is to eradicate gynecologic cancers, and its mission is to promote excellence in the care of women at risk for or affected by gynecologic cancer, achieving this through advocacy, education, research, and interdisciplinary collaboration. And to ensure the organization continues to quickly respond to the evolving needs of its members, it's made it a practice to be data driven in its decision-making process.

The challenge occurs when resources are limited and volunteers express a desire to accomplish numerous goals. To keep the staff and volunteers focused on what the organization is uniquely positioned to deliver, SGO's CEO Pierre Désy, MPH, CAE, evaluates the feasibility of new initiatives and looks for opportunities to collaborate. When there is an opportunity to partner with another organization, SGO embraces it. "Ultimately, our vision is to eradicate women's cancer. We want to work with our members and other organizations to advance the field and improve patient outcomes and research. That is our differentiator. We don't just focus on the needs of our physician members, but the focus is on achieving the mission. Everything we do, the end goal is about patient outcomes."

To narrow the selection of initiatives it is able to undertake and to be nimble and responsive to member needs, SGO relies heavily on data and

CONTINUED ON NEXT PAGE

CONTINUED FROM PREVIOUS PAGE

member feedback. Although the organization operates with a budget of less than $6 million, it collects and disseminates a major study on the state of the practice. The organization also conducts multiple surveys to gather member feedback to ensure it is able to stay ahead of trends and address concerns before they become major challenges and obstacles. To accomplish these tasks with a limited staff, SGO relies on outside assistance. Désy said, "We are okay with hiring external consultants because I can't constantly change the staff. The impact is too great. Working in collaboration is the best approach. We don't use the word 'department,' and we don't work in silos. To me, that is very important and is one of the keys to successfully being able to pivot when needed." Being nimble and agile isn't always about the technology. It is also about how and where you dedicate your resources to ensure you are capable of shifting based on the data you've collected.

Trust

> **"The means are as important as the ends. ... To get things done in ways that destroy trust is not only shortsighted and counterproductive; it is ultimately unsustainable."**
> —Stephen Covey[12]

From the moment you leave your house each morning to the moment you arrive at work, you trust a steady stream of strangers to act and behave in a manner that allows you to accomplish a variety of tasks. If these individuals do not perform in the manner you expect, there may be few—if any—real consequences. Regardless, you plan your day based on your expectations of others' behavior.

For example, imagine your daily routine includes stopping at Starbucks on your way to work. If you visit the coffeehouse during the early morning rush, you will most likely stand behind four or five other patrons before giving the barista your order (unless you use the convenient app to place and pay for your order ahead of time). After paying for your Grande Americano, you walk to the end of the counter and wait for your order to be announced. Throughout this process, you trust that someone will not cut in front of you in line or purposely take your order instead of his or her own. You trust that the container labeled no-fat or low-fat milk does not contain whole milk. If you are carrying a cup of coffee and pass another patron on your way out of the coffeehouse, you expect the patron to give you a little room so that you won't spill hot coffee all over yourself. If you are a new customer or a frequent customer who wishes to try something new, you may even trust the advice of strangers to help you customize your order.

Although there may be an occasional mishap, for the most part, you expect the experience of getting your morning cup of coffee to be the same every day. In fact, you can set your alarm based on this level of trust and feel confident that you'll arrive to work on time even with this reliance on strangers. Familiarity and routine help build trust, as do knowledge and expectation of social norms. In fact, you can travel to a different city in another state and go through the same scenario with a local coffeehouse, and you can expect a similar experience. You may not know if the line will be longer at certain times of the day, but your level of trust is no different even if the venue changes.

Trust and an understanding of the roles and responsibilities of the people you interact with are essential to accomplishing tasks. The bigger the task or initiative, the more vital for both sides to trust and have set expectations. As relationships and levels of trust deepen, you may be more willing to try something new and even risk failure because you know how others will respond.

So it is with associations and the relationship between volunteer leaders and the staff or between the national organization and its chapters or component societies. Associations cannot reverse a trend of declining membership, revenue, or engagement if there is no trust and under-standing between the individuals who set the organization's strategic direction and those asked to implement the strategies and tactics.

Creating Trust through Stakeholder Equality

As your organization aligns its values with its business goals, consider the real obstacles and challenges your organization will face when it comes time to make changes. For some organizations, one of the biggest challenges they face is letting go of employees who have performed well in their job, but their skills no longer align with the needs of the organization.

Soon after becoming CEO at the American Industrial Hygiene Association (AIHA) in 2008, Peter O'Neil, FASAE, CAE, made it a top priority to build a culture that encompasses the values of diversity, inclusion, trust, and transparency and that was aligned with its business goals. To foster a culture that allowed the association to take risks, it was crucial that the association compile a team with the right skill set. If the staff did not believe they could take risks, the organization would never adapt to a rapidly changing environment with new needs and interests. As O'Neil said, "Culture absolutely matters. The what and the how matter. It's the only way you can get new ideas through. Sometimes the skill gap is too wide, and you need to train or hire new staff or shift responsibilities. I need to employ folks where we have a hand-and-glove fit. In some cases, the relationship works until it doesn't. When that happens, you have to address it. I've seen too many organizations allow staff to continue in a role that no longer fits their skill set or that they've outgrown. Culture makes or breaks us."

Founded in 1939, AIHA is one of the largest international associations serving occupational and environmental health and safety professionals practicing industrial hygiene, and it is a resource for those in large corporations and small businesses, as well as those who work independently as consultants. Although the organization had successfully navigated the many changes that occurred in the workforce during the 20th century, it became clear that AIHA needed to expand into new areas to remain relevant. With that goal in mind and with a vision of a world of safe and trusted products, the idea behind the Product Stewardship Society was conceived. The Product Stewardship Society enables professionals to promote responsible design, development, and management of products throughout their lifecycles. The reason it was created, however, was to provide a home for product steward professionals. Although other organizations meet the needs of professionals involved in different aspects of the product lifecycle in this industry, those organizations were not as comprehensive in scope.

O'Neil credits AIHA's ability to launch the new society to trust. Everyone involved in the development, launch, and management of the society trusted each other. All stakeholders had an equal voice, from the board to the CEO to the staff. The staff members trusted the board that if they failed in their efforts, they wouldn't be fired or reprimanded. According to O'Neil, "the only reason they were willing to do this was because we have a 'speak with one voice' culture. People have a voice, and those voices are equally respected. That doesn't mean that if we have consensus we have unanimity. Even if I wasn't in favor of something, I feel that my voice was heard. We had a strong culture, a level of trust for each other. The board knew that we would do the best we could." By creating an environment built on trust, the organization could take risks and try new ideas, which ultimately would lead to a greater likelihood of being relevant in the future. If the world didn't change, this wouldn't be necessary. But there isn't a market where everything functions exactly the way it has for the past few decades, let alone the past 100 years.

Taking risks and building trust require accountability. When O'Neil first arrived at AIHA, the relationship between the board and staff was dysfunctional. Staff were less likely to suggest new approaches or test new ideas because they did not believe they would be fully supported by the volunteer leadership. To mitigate the risk and increase the level of confidence between volunteer leaders and staff, O'Neil made a stronger commitment to collecting the data leaders and staff needed to feel comfortable with their decisions. In addition, when mistakes were made, "We'd own it," O'Neil said. "When you have accountability and responsibility, it becomes pride, and you build a sense that we are all in this together. I created an atmosphere in which people feel completely heard." Creating such an atmosphere included engaging younger and less experienced members of the staff in the conversation. "They tend to see things very differently than more senior-level staff. I then combined the input and shared it with our leaders."

Moving forward O'Neil believes that to be competitive and relevant in the future, organizations need to embrace the 21st century notion of diversity and inclusion and weave that into the fabric of the organization. As organizations embrace change and take risks, they must adapt their delivery channels to ensure they incorporate the key characteristics of a successful business model, including accessibility and affordability. It's not only about innovating the product line; it's also about how you deliver. You need diversity of thought to update the product lines, as well as the different channels used to reach a more diverse audience.

Diversity and Inclusion as a Business Strategy

Say the words *diversity and inclusion* and the natural inclination, if you were born before 1980, is to interpret it as focusing on *representation* and *fairness.* At least that is a conclusion of a 2015 study produced by the Billie Jean King Leadership Initiative and the Deloitte University Leadership Center for Inclusion. By comparison, when millennials are asked about diversity, they tend to focus on unique experiences and suggest the purpose of creating programs aimed at diversity and inclusion should be on improved business outcomes. The study, which examined issues impacting the current workforce, found that members of generation X and baby boomers use identifiers such as gender, race, ethnicity, and sexual orientation to define diversity and argue that businesses should focus on expanding efforts to diversify because it is the "right thing to do." The millennial definition, on the other hand, focuses on differences in experiences, viewpoints, knowledge, and insights.[13] As one millennial survey respondent said, "Diversity is a variety of cultures and perspectives working together to solve business problems."[14]

To address the challenges many associations face in their efforts to provide value and be relevant to a variety of audiences and individuals with varying backgrounds, many organizations are increasing their focus on diversity and inclusion. And connecting these efforts to business outcomes increases the likelihood of helping associations expand their reach.

One of the leading voices on diversity and inclusion in the association community is Velma Hart, FASAE, CAE, veteran, former ASAE chairperson, and chief financial officer for numerous nonprofit organizations. She described diversity in business in broad terms: "In business planning, one of the fundamental aspects is expand your horizon. As organizations make efforts to expand their reach, they don't always include the opinions of different voices. Organizations used to target one customer to the exclusion of others. Now that the population with discretionary income is greater, if you want to sell a product or change an outcome, you want to make sure you get every perspective available. It's not just about race, gender, and religion. Some organizations are just trying to change the face of the business, believing that is a driver. But you want someone with a different experience or knowledge base and who sees things differently. That is what diversity is in business."

Hart believes the old way of making decisions—bringing together the senior leaders of the profession—is passé. Instead, she recommends including individuals who can help frame a discussion and identify solutions from a wider range of experiences, knowledge, and tenure. However, in order for them to fully contribute, they must be treated as equals. Hart added, "The old titles shouldn't exist—we want the best and brightest minds at the table regardless of how they rank."

Many organizations strive for diversity and inclusion yet remain fixated on a definition that reflects an older generation rather than the generation they wish to reach. When younger members of the workforce are invited to serve on committees, they are often the lone voice in a sea of experienced members and may not be treated as an equal among peers but as a nod to a diversity and inclusion initiative.

Hart further argued, "To make change, diversity manifests itself as different ways of thinking. Approach it differently. Sometimes it's driven by people, information, and how you collect it. Organizations need to consider who and what community they ask to engage on a topic." As you work to increase diversity and inclusion within your organization, give some thought to building a coalition of stakeholders representing a variety of backgrounds, experiences, and approaches to solving common problems. Include your biggest critics and your newest members to ensure you are surrounding yourself with individuals who will help the organization rethink its approach to meeting the needs of your community and the profession.

CHAPTER 3

●

Culture

"Culture needs to take strategy out to lunch."
—David Gammel, CEO, Entomological Society of America

Netflix: See What's Next. Watch Anywhere. Cancel Anytime.

Netflix is often credited for creating a disruptive innovation that resulted in a better delivery of movies and original content. The term *disruptive innovation* was first used by Clayton Christensen to describe "a process by which a product or service takes root initially in simple applications at the bottom of a market and then relentlessly moves up market, eventually displacing established competitors."[1] Netflix's first customers were drawn to its differentiating value proposition: no late fees and the convenience of ordering online and having movies delivered directly to your home at no additional cost. It provided an alternative to Blockbuster by focusing on the biggest pain point and solving an issue that many consumers frequently struggled with—returning movies in a timely manner.

However, it also disrupted its own business model when it transitioned from mailing DVDs to online video streaming. As access to faster internet speeds and mobile devices shifted the preferred format for viewing content, Netflix quickly made the shift to online streaming. In doing so, it abandoned an infrastructure that included a warehouse of movies, printed

47

mailing envelopes, and a staff trained for jobs specific to this approach. The move to online streaming, however, enabled the company to deliver content on-demand to anyone, anywhere in the world who maintains a subscription.

While at its core, Netflix is in the business of creating and delivering content, its business model is centered around the concept of flexibility—available anywhere, cancel anytime. To accomplish this, Netflix promotes its culture as one that includes primarily "A Team" professionals, individuals who work hard and perform at the highest level. If an individual underperforms or his skill set no longer meets the needs of the job (even if he was a top performer), he will soon find himself unemployed.

In a "Culture Deck" that has been viewed more than 17 million times[2] and called, "the most important document ever to come out of the [Silicon] Valley" by Facebook COO, Sheryl Sandberg[3], Netflix adheres to five main principles to describe its unusual culture. On the company's website in the jobs section, it states, "What is special about Netflix, though, is how much we

1. Encourage independent decision making by employees
2. Share information openly, broadly, and deliberately
3. Are extraordinarily candid with each other
4. Keep only our highly effective people
5. Avoid rules"

Since it opened its doors more than two decades ago, Netflix's approach to hiring employees and using the best infrastructure needed to support its business goals has remained constant in that it continually evolves.

Netflix is unafraid to radically change the organization if that is what's needed to achieve the mission. By contrast, many associations believe the bigger risk is making major changes to their staff, their product/program portfolios, and their infrastructures. Interestingly enough, compared to many for-profit companies, associations have more opportunity to function like Netflix because their missions should not keep them chained to a particular type of content or delivery channel. The programs, products, and services an association delivers should only be maintained as long as they serve the mission and meet the needs of its audience.

And while Netflix has made some missteps along the way and not every idea has been a success, this appears to be part of the formula for Netflix's success, as evidenced by a statement made by CEO Reed Hastings during a 2017 technology conference: "Our hit ratio is too high right now. We have to take more risks ... to try more crazy things ... we should have a higher cancel rate overall."[4] This sentiment echoes a viewpoint I heard repeatedly from the association leaders I interviewed: fail fast and learn.

As appealing as Netflix culture may be to some organizations, it isn't the right fit for everyone. As Jamie Notter, author of *Culture That Works: How Getting Serious About Culture Unlocks New Performance,* said during an interview with me, "We've consistently been missing the mark by viewing culture as ideal rather than tailoring to the market." Similar to how there isn't one business model that will fit every organization, culture needs to be aligned with an organization's goals. On page two of Notter's book he says, "Culture is not about being cool or even about having happy employees. It is about reinforcing what drives the success of the enterprise and subsequently being able to adapt the culture ... as markets and internal dynamics shift."

As organizations shift their business models or pivot their approaches to achieving their missions, they cannot overlook the importance of having the right culture to achieve their goals. And regardless of the culture they create, at its core there must be trust, respect, and accountability.

Harnessing the Passion, Talent, and Skills of Your Staff

At the American Institute of Architects (AIA), people are central to what the organization does. Although the organization had a set of stated values, its staff culture did not reflect the statements it had been using to define the work environment. As Catherine Wemette, CAE, Director of Employee Learning and Engagement at AIA, phrased it, "We had organizational values, but no one knew about them. We found them, dusted them off, and they were exactly what you would imagine." To better align the staff culture with the organizational values, Wemette and her team focused on leveraging the interests and strengths of the staff. "We redefined our approach to ensure the AIA was a better place to work by focusing on ways to harness the passion, talents, and skills of staff. We borrowed the phrase *Hamsterdam* to define our internal efforts to encourage staff to pursue projects about which they're passionate. Its origins come from a reference to applying new approaches to the same old problems." The Hamsterdam Core team is a select group of AIA employees charged with supporting positive culture change at AIA. In 2016, the core team led efforts to redefine staff values centered on people, passion, design, and the future.

Recognizing the need to engage other individuals in efforts to support an inclusive and productive work environment, AIA created HamsterdamX. The cross-teams, or Xteams, are open to everyone on staff at AIA and cover a variety of interest areas. For example, the Outreach team rallies both AIA headquarters staff and local partners to host charitable campaigns benefitting the greater Washington, DC, community. The group promotes AIA's Philanthropic Leave Policy and plans donation drives. The Lunch and Learn team brings in a variety of speakers to share new ideas and ways of thinking with staff to support the values on an ongoing basis. And the Equity and Inclusion team seeks to celebrate the diversity of experiences, backgrounds, and talents that make AIA a strong and vibrant community.

Developing a culture that aligns with the organization's values is not an easy task. In fact, it can be so challenging that many organizations ignore it to focus on strategy, or they copy another organization's culture, believing that imitation will lead to matching achievements. This approach comes from a misunderstanding of what an organizational culture should be. In *Culture That Works*, Notter defines culture as "the collection of things that clarifies and reinforces what is really valued by the system."[5] Notter argues that because the point of culture is to "drive the success of the enterprise,"[6] once you focus on culture, you can help your organization gain a competitive advantage. Defining your organization's business model and what is valued should go hand-in-hand with building a culture that will support your goals. If an association's board or staff fear failure or if they avoid taking risks because the culture is risk-adverse, it is unlikely they will innovate or adapt in time to remain relevant and meet the needs of the members and customers they serve.

AIA Values

AIA Staff Values

- People are central to what we do.
- We are passionate about our work.
- We believe in the power of design.
- We have a bright future.

What does this look like?

- *People are central to what we do.*
  - We strive to understand and support our members and the work they do.
  - We assume positive intentions and have each other's backs.
  - We pursue clarity and accountability through open, consistent, and direct communication.
  - We are responsive and honest, treating everyone with respect independent of status or disagreement.
  - We listen with empathy, identify root causes, and respond appropriately.
  - We value diversity of thought and the unique contributions we each make to our mission.

- *We are passionate about our work.*
  - We approach each project, initiative, and issue with the member in mind.
  - We are engaged in and enthusiastic about our work.
  - We enjoy challenges, celebrate our successes together, and use our mistakes to learn and change.
  - We take the opportunity to do our best every day.
  - We think big and have fun.

CONTINUED ON NEXT PAGE

CONTINUED FROM PREVIOUS PAGE

- **We believe in the power of design.**
  - We provide opportunities to learn about architecture's value, history, utility, and impact.
  - We pursue excellence for ourselves, our communities, and our world.
  - We look for solutions that work right, look right, and feel right.

- **We have a bright future.**
  - We share a focus on moving the Institute forward.
  - We strive for solutions in an empowered, collaborative environment.
  - We seek opportunities to grow as individuals and as an organization by trying new things and taking smart risks.
  - We invest in the tools and resources to lead successfully.
  - We support our members in making a difference in the world.

Abandon Management-by-Anecdote To Help Increase Relevancy

When Chris Gloede was hired by the American Bar Association as its first chief marketing officer, he understood the organization had three primary goals: grow membership, increase representation, and reduce the organization's marketing spend. Prior to Gloede's arrival, the American Bar's marketing, customer service, data management, sales, and research departments were siloed. Gloede's position marked the first time the 100-person team responsible for nearly $80 million in annual revenue was organized under a single leader with a common mission: create a consistent, branded, cross-customer experience.

Driving the change was a growing sense of irrelevance. Legal practices were reportedly operating under tighter budgets and smaller client revenues. As demands to increase billable hours grew, many lawyers were either unwilling or unable to travel to national conferences. And for-profit competition vied for lawyers' time and attention by providing legal resources and continuing legal education online for free or at highly discounted rates. As the next generation entered the workforce, they appeared less inclined to join a large national organization if it did not provide relevant value at a good price.

Internally at American Bar, the barriers to achieving goals were just as large. Staff were neither rewarded for positive results nor critiqued for poor performance. Some initiatives were led by individuals who had been promoted to leadership positions but did not have the business experience, knowledge, or skills needed to succeed. When strategies were developed, they were often based on anecdotes rather than research and data.

Although the American Bar is the largest community of lawyers in the world and provides education, publications, and opportunities to network and volunteer, the organization was following a strategy that enabled it to function but was holding it back from growth. Over time, if it did not address the internal issues and develop a sustainable business model to engage a changing market, it could see a steady decline in market share.

Gloede's team realized to better meet the needs of today's lawyers, it would need to eliminate products, services, and programs with low participation that could not be scaled in a cost-effective manner. Gloede said, "We had a team of four staff working on a product that was high in quality but underutilized. With 400,000 members, we needed national products that reach tens of thousands, not dozens." Gloede added, "It was a favorite program of some, but the market showed no demand. We reallocated the resources to areas that had a need and demand."

The organization also needed to offer new products that were accessible, affordable, and relevant. At its core, the business model focused on leveraging existing strengths and expanding internal capabilities. With a reputation for delivering high-quality education, books, and career resources, the American Bar launched a new monthly continuing legal education program, attracting an average of 20,000 or more attendees. And the publishing department expanded its sales channels with Amazon and relaunched the state bar book promotion program.

Gloede further explained, "Society changes, law changes, people change. And so, the American Bar must also change to continue meeting the needs of those we serve. As a national business with deep volumes of content, products, and services, we have a short moment to match our offerings to our customer needs. To succeed, we must abandon management by anecdote and embrace the power of technology and data to grow our retail and social service work."

The American Bar is not only a national organization; it also includes specialty divisions and forums that develop content. Gloede noted, "I had to navigate the waters and find the white space that wasn't under control, the zones where you can play in, and it's difficult to do that research. It's intuition and research—50/50. The biggest thing we needed to do was to fail fast. We needed to launch a quality product but also confirm there was market demand." If Gloede and his team found the market demand to be strong enough, they could funnel additional resources into the product and try to expand its reach.

When he arrived at the American Bar, the culture did not favor risk and failure. Gloede made the following observation: "These are lawyers, a combative group. If you screw up, you hear it. I took it on the chin. We had to take and try something new. I had to build a culture with staff who took risks and knew I supported them."

Once the American Bar developed a stronger value proposition, it was in a better position to grow its membership. The new approach to recruitment focused on improved social media tactics, increased personalization, and simplified messaging. The American Bar also created a free student member category and built a lead generation program. Most importantly, the American Bar invested in digital content, updated its technology stack, and launched its new e-commerce site for more than 1,000 products. To compete in today's market, Gloede recognized the importance of providing value and delivering it in a way that makes it more accessible and affordable.

To improve the American Bar's ability to leverage customer insights, Gloede invested resources and time into validating its database. "Once we knew the data was valid, we could better target our messages to the right population and increase personalization."

Improving the value proposition and investing in a better technology stack would not deliver the results it was seeking if staff skills were not upgraded in the process. From creating individualized training plans for high performers to updating all job descriptions with minimum acceptable qualifications, Gloede better aligned goals and initiatives with the individuals assigned to assist in the implementation.

Changes to staff roles, responsibilities, and expectations require a fanatical focus on the end result—making the customer happy. When Gloede first arrived at the American Bar, it was immediately obvious that most staff were not ready for a change. Gloede observed, "Associations are not the corporate world. The culture is supportive of staff, sometimes over outcomes." The next role Gloede needed to step into was as a micro-mentor. Different from a micromanager who tells staff what to do and how to do it, Gloede spent the majority of his day during the first few years helping staff identify problems, look for solutions, and implement new approaches. At night, he worked on the strategy elements. At a certain point, he knew it was time to realign staff to better meet the needs of the new strategy. One of the gaps that needed filling was an analytics department. Gloede identified individuals who could be better used in other areas and expanded the leadership team within the affinity and membership areas.

Gloede stated, "One of the challenges associations have is focusing too much on a leader or vocal member. They don't always have a focus on the customer. They focus on the board, who is more experienced, more engaged. But that is not the average customer, and that is not customer focused. The American Bar has 450,000 customers; you need the reporting and research to understand the customer journey and personas to build product development. The board is not your customer. They shouldn't be directing the product. Everything we did at the organization is performance-based. Every Tuesday morning, I reviewed the reports, circled what didn't make sense, and gave it to my staff to get feedback on what needed to change." Leaders need to understand that the focus is on the member or customer, not the volunteer leadership or staff. Moreover, many organizations want change, but they don't want *to* change. However, to succeed in the long run, organizations need to change, fail, and recover.

Lessons Learned From the American Bar Association

1. Listen to a representative collection of members' voices. Most associations' boards are not representative of their members or customers. Even if one or two early career professionals serve on the board, if they don't have an influential voice, their contributions and opinions may be ignored. While some organizations acknowledge their boards do not represent the variances in the market, very few rely upon industry research and consumer behavior to help make decisions. The voice of the member cannot be heard if an organization relies too heavily on responding to the board's concerns and opinions and not enough time listening to the customer. To improve your board's decision-making process, it's equally important to invest time and resources into a centralized database that integrates all member and customer sales and engagements. Using a combination of research and purchasing data, organizations can improve their decision-making process regarding when to stop offering a product and when to invest in new ones.

2. Establish a process for regularly assessing your offerings. If the three main barriers to engagement—access, time, and money—are not addressed, organizations will eventually experience a decline in sales and find it difficult to maintain or grow their market share. Think about initiatives that some consider important but don't deliver results. Nearly every organization preserves products and programs that should be retired because they 1) are no longer profitable, 2) no longer serve the needs of its intended audience, or 3) are not easy to access and use. Often this occurs because they rely too heavily on anecdotes and the opinions of a select group of highly engaged members. Once these programs become an opportunity cost, the organization will be limited in taking on new initiatives. At least once a year, an organization's portfolio of programs, products, and services should be evaluated to ensure it continues to provide enough value to a sizeable percentage of members and customers. The list of products should include conferences, tradeshows, events, publications, tools, certifications, affinity programs, and any other offering that requires an investment of staff time and resources.

a. Set a minimum performance standard for all product lines. Performance should include participation and profitability. Does it break even after expenses?

b. If a product drops below minimum standards, use research to determine the product's level of relevance within key markets. Is the target market shrinking or growing? Are there competitors that provide a more accessible or affordable product? If the product were to be discontinued, where would members and customers turn for a replacement?

c. If the product is still relevant to a large enough audience, look for opportunities to update or improve it through new distribution channels or partners. This may include outsourcing publications to a new publisher, using Amazon for book sales, or identifying a new affinity partner that may provide a better solution.

d. If the product is no longer relevant to a large enough audience, sunset the program and reinvest the time and resources into a new product that might better meet the needs of your target audience.

e. Once you've identified a new product or program, plan to fail fast, identify what can be improved, and relaunch the product quickly. This will require setting standards to evaluate a product's performance during each stage of its growth. New products rarely achieve similar levels of use as those that have been in the marketplace and have built a strong user base. Many new programs and products may experience a loss in revenue in year one, break even in year two, and become profitable by year three. Regardless of how the new product performs, the team should continue to evaluate customer satisfaction and likelihood to recommend the product (e.g., Net Promoter Score) and should examine if the product is being accessed by its intended audience.

f. Results matter, but accountability is necessary to learn from positive or negative results. Accountability means learning from any failures.

3. Ensure staff have the skills they need to help your organization succeed. Organizations must invest in keeping staff skills updated and in aligning

job roles and responsibilities with knowledge and abilities. Although associations are in the business of providing continuing education and training to their members, many fall behind when it comes to ensuring their staffs have what it takes to succeed in their jobs. Just as results and accountability matter when determining if you should grow, invest, or divest in products, the same is true for staff performance. When your organization updates its technology stack, it must also ensure staff have the training they need to succeed. At times, this may require hiring new staff and letting others go, including those who may have excelled at a previous position but are not the best fit for a new role. By setting goals, providing staff with the training and technology they need, and holding them accountable, your organization should be well positioned to increase overall performance and provide more value to members and customers.

Culture That Works by Jamie Notter

In his 2017 book *Culture That Works: How Getting Serious About Culture Unlocks New Performance*, Notter explains that organizations can be caught off guard when the culture that helped them achieve past success no longer provides what is needed to thrive in the future. "Culture is about what is deeply valued in the system, and—here's the important part—making sure what is valued is connected to what drives success for the enterprise."[7] As the situation or environment in which the organization operates changes, it's essential to keep the culture in alignment. If the organizational culture is not adapted to be compatible with the goals and plans of the company, "in most cases it's the culture that wins and the plans (and results) that lose."

Notter gives the example of two core values many organizations express: 1) dedication to customer service and 2) prioritization of long-term strategy. While both ideas represent good values, in practice they can create a contradictory culture. Customer service often requires quickly responding to needs, concerns, or questions, while focusing on strategy requires thoughtful planning beyond the immediate needs of members or customers. When a situation arises that creates a tug-of-war between these two values, the organization needs to find a balance that produces results. It's about connecting cultural values to the success of the business.

4. Synchronize your organization's volunteer leadership with staff to accomplish goals. Too often, decisions are delayed because the governing board meets infrequently. A successful business plan can be the guide for executing the board's strategy. Some of the decisions within the business plan should be made by staff. If there is a culture of trust between the staff and volunteer leadership, staff will be able to make decisions, take risks, and adapt or change course when needed, and thus they are more likely to feel invested in their jobs. Your organization's volunteer leadership must find the balance between accountability and trust if it wishes to adapt and grow at the rapid pace of change.

Becoming Agile

When it comes to making a decision to purchase a product online, speed and efficiency are essential. As a consumer placing an order online, you expect it to arrive on your doorstep within a day or two. The speed of delivery matters for most consumers, and they will make a purchase decision based on how quickly they can access or receive the item they have ordered. Responding to the need to deliver products quickly often requires an increase in costs, and therefore efficiency becomes an important attribute in how goods are designed, created, and delivered. Although most people don't think about the process of supply chain management, its effect on purchase behavior, loyalty, and profitability is significant—and it's constantly evolving.

Although a number of organizations serve many of the vertical industries in the supply chain process, with more than 45,000 members in 100 countries, APICS is considered one of the largest organizations serving the end-to-end supply chain profession. To achieve its goals, more than 2,000 active volunteers and 100 staff work together to deliver high-quality education, information, and certifications. The story behind the growth and the successful transformation of the association and the industry began in 2006. But the association continues to transform to meet changes in its industry. During the first decade of the 21st century, the organization was shrinking despite the growth within the profession. To address the challenges and leverage the untapped opportunities, APICS hired Abe Eshkenazi, CSCP, CPA, FASAE, CAE, as its chief executive officer.

While improvements were being made to the design, planning, execution, control, and monitoring of supply chain activities and the profession was being elevated to a more strategic role within many large companies, APICS saw its membership decline from 72,000 to 42,000. Internally, the staff felt rudderless because the strategic priorities of the organization changed almost annually. The content produced by the organization had become outdated, and the board of directors assumed an operational role rather than a strategic one. Because board members had limited terms, there was little consistency or direction. Projects were frequently started but not completed. Although the situation created a crisis, the lack of trust between APICS staff and board ultimately became the biggest obstacle that needed to be removed if the organization was to align itself with the market. An assessment of the past actions and performance of the board made it clear that it lacked a strategic focus, spending more of its time on operational issues rather than creating and following a multiyear strategic plan.

To address the issues facing the organization, Eshkenazi's first goal was to develop a new sense of trust between the board and the staff. Eshkenazi explained, "First, we had to create a strategic plan based on where the board saw opportunities for growth within the market. Second, we assured the board that the priorities they set would be followed and executed upon. We were held accountable to achieving the goals in the strategic plan. We wanted the board to know that if they ask for something, they were going to get it. No other priorities could be set. This would give the staff direction and build the trust needed to execute the plan. We needed trust with staff and board. We are all aligned—no deviation."

Once the board and staff were aligned, APICS began to chart a course that would help it grow and thrive well into the future. And then, the Great Recession hit the United States and caused a prolonged economic downturn. Eshkenazi recalled, "It had a significant effect on our members. APICS's revenues declined by approximately 20 percent, and we had to lay off staff, due to no fault of their own." The situation forced the organization to once again examine its governance model, its business model, and its value proposition, leading to its next transformation—to be an "end-to-end, from design to workforce development, supply chain management association." The concept of end-to-end guided a business decision to grow through mergers and acquisitions. Because the board was now functioning at a strategic rather than operational level, it understood the importance of transforming the organization to better reflect the changes going on within the industry.

APICS's board not only embraced transformation through new business and governance models, but also it now viewed governance review as an activity it should conduct yearly. "We do not shy away from governance conversations," Eshkenazi explained. "That will drive this organization to the future. We need the appropriate mix of individuals serving on this board. They set the vision, and we translate that into priorities. We are completely aligned in terms of their expectations." When APICS considers changes to its business model, it is the result of seeing a new market opportunity. Eshkenazi added, "We treat and view APICS as a business. There is no such thing as not-for-profit. We are a tax-exempt organization. We drive profit in order to reinvest in our programs, products, and services."

In today's market, Eshkenazi firmly believes the organization must be able to compete at every level. From e-commerce to omnichannel distribution, the organization must embrace the disruptions in the industry. And this can only occur if the association is agile. "We need to move faster than the current business model allows us. The changes in the marketplace are not waiting for us to adopt and adapt; they are moving around us. Associations cannot take nine months to make a decision."

With a high level of trust between the volunteer leaders and the staff and the willingness to make major changes to ensure alignment with a rapidly changing environment, APICS is well positioned to once again change its business model. Not one to rest on past performance and ignore the signs that the current model may not be sustainable in the future, Eshkenazi is preparing the organization to respond to changing market demands for content. In 2018, 30 percent of APICS revenue is derived from its original content or body of knowledge that is used to prepare for industry certification programs. However, as major universities, including the Massachusetts Institute of Technology and Stanford, begin to offer the content for free through massive open online courses, there is a high likelihood that individuals will no longer be willing to pay for the content offered by APICS. Eshkenazi believes the entire association model, from membership to in-person conferences, will experience a seismic shift as competitors such as LinkedIn and other for-profit companies leverage their databases and as individuals look for more digital experiences. "Our competition will come from nontraditional sources. Schools are now developing supply-chain knowledge. In 1995, only six schools offered degrees in the discipline. Now there are more than 500 schools with a supply chain management program," said Eshkenazi.

Supporting Trends in Education from *ASAE ForesightWorks*

- "Massive open online course offerings and participation continue to grow as the MOOC model is refined."[8]

- "Microlearning is becoming increasingly popular for corporate training, in part because the format can be readily adapted to meet the growing demand for training content on mobile devices."

- "The number and types of credentials beyond traditional academic degrees are rising."

Despite the threat of competition and the extinction of a major revenue source for the organization, Eshkenazi is optimistic about APICS's future. "I thrive on change. I have to be careful to pull back and allow the management team to pause. Adopt and adapt for now. I need to be careful on how much change I push." When APICS leadership sees a challenge, it becomes an opportunity. It's not unusual for the organization to test new ideas and fail. Eshkenazi explained, "Internally, if we are not failing, we are not succeeding. If we are succeeding at everything, we are not taking enough chances. Learn, adapt, and move forward. The board is comfortable with that. The only way to get better is by trying. We are willing to take on an activity. The metaphor we are using is this: we are flying a plane—with passengers, staff, board, and everyone—and we need to rebuild it while it's flying. We can't land it. We need to rebuild it from the back, with multiple stakeholders sitting on the plane who all have an influence on what you do."

APICS plans to pivot again, from primarily serving the individuals who work in the profession to the organizations that employ them. After the recession, APICS had to adapt its value proposition and how it communicated the benefits of membership to meet the needs of the employer. APICS leadership understands that if their focus doesn't enhance the organizations that employ their members, financial support will wane. APICS's focus is now squarely on organizational success through the individual. "We are as concerned about the output as about the development of the individual," said Eshkenazi.

Years ago, many individuals thrived in the business world as functional experts. Today, having functional expertise is what you need to get an entry-level position. Companies want individuals with management and leadership skills. Being able to lead initiatives and having cross-functional expertise are essential to career advancement. Although training and education are ubiquitous (and soon it may even be free and accessible to anyone seeking the information), there is an opportunity for associations to fill the leadership training gap within the professions they serve. The speed of change requires associations to be nimble and adapt at a rate they have never had to in the past. If associations do not close this gap, other organizations will take advantage of the opening in the marketplace. In the case of APICS, the organization served its members by helping them gain the skills they needed to succeed in the changing business environment.

Looking back across the past 10 years, Eshkenazi believes the two most important components to the successful transformation of the organization were the establishment of a trust-based relationship between the board and the staff and hiring the right people.

> **"I treat people as human beings .... If they know**
> **you care, it brings out the best in them."**
> —Sir Richard Branson, founder of the Virgin Group[9]

Lessons Learned From APICS

1. Build and maintain a high level of trust between volunteer leaders
   and staff. It is a cultural component that is essential to the success of
   an organization. When trust between the two parties exists, it builds
   accountability and supports a culture unafraid to take risks. It has been
   my observation that organizations with high levels of trust between
   volunteer leaders and the staff are more likely to meet and exceed goals.
   Ask yourself:

   a. Do volunteer leaders demonstrate their respect for staff? It is
      the minor conversations and acknowledgements or the tone of
      communication that provide the best opportunity to demonstrate
      respect for each other. Trust that is created as the result of small
      interactions may become defining moments for building successful
      relationships between the two groups.

   b. How transparent is the organization after decisions are made by
      the board and the staff is instructed to execute on the initiatives?
      When the board makes strategic decisions that change the roles
      and responsibilities of staff—or even may lead to a reorganization
      of staff roles—is it fully transparent on how the decision was made
      and what it hopes to accomplish? One of the best, and often fastest,
      ways to build trust is through transparency. If your staff members
      are unable to complete the initiatives identified in the strategic
      plan, are they transparent about the obstacles that stood in their
      way?

2. Pay attention to trends, even if they are not yet impacting your industry.
   By paying attention to the trend of free education through massive open
   online courses, for example, APICS can identify an alternative way to
   provide relevant education before a decline in registrations for its traditional programs affects its revenue. Keep in mind the likelihood that
   trends influencing how consumers interact with other organizations

will spill over to their relationships with professional associations. If your organization is not planning ahead and paying attention to trends before they hit your bottom line, you'll be in an uphill battle trying to find your place as the go-to source of continuing education and information. And members will turn to other sources for solutions if an organization is unable to meet their needs or if another organization offers a similar program or product for free. To be nimble and respond to changes in the market, organizations must pay attention to trends and be able to pivot when needed.

   a. Do you routinely monitor and track trends that may impact your organization, your members, and your relevancy?

   b. Do you engage members of your board and your staff in helping to identify trends that may change how your organization makes money and engages with members and customers?

3. Identify and recruit volunteer leaders who fully understand that it is more important to be concerned with the organization as a whole than to represent only the interests of a component or chapter within the organization. This isn't to say that if a board member once served on the board of a chapter that his or her allegiance will remain to the chapter. There will come a time when board members must make decisions that could negatively affect a part of the organization where they previously held strong ties or are currently still connected. Do they view themselves as representatives or the voice of a chapter or component? If they wish to achieve their mission, vision, and strategic goals, organizations must cultivate leaders who will serve the organization first and the interests and needs of their special interest areas or chapters second.

4. Look for problems and pain points within the profession to increase relevance. Problems are simply opportunities waiting to be solved. When viewed through a different lens and embraced by leadership and staff, the organization is more likely to be on a growth trajectory than a fixed one. When problems or challenges pose a potential threat to a major product line or revenue stream, does your organization look at it as an opportunity and consider all possible options, or does it look only for answers that will help it maintain the status quo?

Making a Stellar Brand More Relevant

"Whenever you see a successful business, someone once made a courageous decision."

— commonly attributed to Peter Drucker, management consultant

If you paid a visit to your physician for a check-up within the last few years, you probably noticed a change in how the practice manages appointments, billing, and communication. Health systems have aggressively targeted physician practices as part of their strategy to align physician networks and satisfy payment reforms. And many physicians within the healthcare community have opted-in to the system, becoming employees of a larger institution.[10] The landscape for delivering healthcare is rapidly changing, and medical practices are finding they need to quickly adapt if they are to survive. In years past, physician practices relied heavily on their specialty, sub-specialty, or other professional associations to keep them updated. Today, they have many more sources to keep them informed, including the larger institutions that are acquiring practices as well as for-profit companies that are moving into the healthcare space.

Once a major voice and resource provider to the profession, the Medical Group Management Association (MGMA) found itself maintaining its current member base but not attracting new members or customers as the landscape changed around it. The organization held on to an old business model that focused primarily on the individual member yet failed to provide opportunities for other audiences to engage. At the time Halee Fischer-Wright, MD, MMM, FAAP, FACMPE, was hired as CEO and president, the MGMA brand was well recognized for its compensation study and resources for individuals helping to manage medical practices. According to Fischer-Wright, there has never been a time when medical practices have been more important to the delivery of healthcare. Serving more than 40,000 medical practice group leaders, MGMA is one of the nation's top membership associations dedicated to educating and advocating for the profession. "Our members serve more than 45 percent of healthcare, touching nearly half of the 3.4 billion medical office visits a year. It's a relevant job," said Fischer-Wright.

Across the years, MGMA made a few transitions that paralleled healthcare; however, its general focus remained unchanged. And what worked

10 to 15 years ago was not working in 2013–2015. Fischer-Wright said, "Once you have a diet of making money and being successful and things start to change ... if you haven't been on the forefront of the change, when decline happens you are behind the eight ball. We have a stellar brand, but we needed to make a transition in how we served the entire market." The challenge MGMA faced was how to take an institutional brand and make it market relevant. Similar to other traditional membership organizations, the focus had been on individual members, and the organization needed to pivot to look at the industry.

Fischer-Wright knew within 100 days of arrival what needed to be done for the organization to achieve its mission: Keep an eye on the changing needs of its members, be aware of the trends occurring within the health-care industry, and expand its focus to customers, who in the past garnered little attention. In other words, MGMA needed to know everything it could about the profession, even more than its members, if it was to develop a value proposition that would be relevant in the future.

The first big board meeting could have been Fischer-Wright's last after she shared what she had found during her first 100 days of due diligence. The news wasn't just bad; it was horrible. Although no one wants to hear bad news, after what Fischer-Wright calls the "walk through the valley of the shadow of death" meeting, she understood that the board needed to hear the truth if the organization was going to make a major transition in how it achieved its mission. She recalled, "They needed to hear it. One board member asked how the board would ever trust me. I wouldn't expect the board to have the same intimate knowledge I have, but I was surprised they had ownership over what had happened. I was objective: 'Here is what it is. These are the five things we need to focus on.'" To help the board make decisions, Fischer-Wright made transparency a priority and used data to support the changes that were urgently needed if the organization was to reverse the trend of declining membership and revenue.

To gain the board's trust, Fischer-Wright understood the importance of over-communicating to ensure they stayed informed. She also told them they could hold her accountable to both the successes and failures they may encounter as they shifted from the previous business model to a new one. "If we failed, I promised the board we'd evaluate what happened and make the changes necessary so that it didn't happen again. That's how we built trust with the board. One of my goals as the CEO is to make the board successful."

One thing was immediately obvious to Fischer-Wright: if the organization hoped to move forward, it would require a different style of leadership. It required a compelling story of why revenue matters to the mission. For many nonprofit board members, this isn't intuitive. "We used to say no margin, no mission. For a lot of associations, that was new thinking or different thinking. It required a change in perspective. That was the transformation we were leading at MGMA," Fischer-Wright explained.

Change is hard, both for the board of directors and for the staff. The individuals who were serving on the board when Fischer-Wright became the CEO had been moving up through the leadership ranks for 20 years. Many had been trained to believe the organization should focus only on initiatives that served the membership—that profit margins were not part of the equation. To all of a sudden have a business philosophy change, even if the importance of the shift was explained, was hard for many board members to align with their beliefs. "It's a tightrope act," said Fischer-Wright. "As a new CEO, you don't want to be at odds with your board, and you need to build trust and transparency. In my heart I knew that if they didn't choose a new path, they wouldn't be around. That was a good platform to work from. That was the burning platform. You don't want to be the last leader of a 90-year-old organization. That haunts me every single day."

One of the first issues Fischer-Wright tackled was the lack of trust between the board and the senior leadership team that preceded her in this role. "The only way to develop trust is to be transparent, show why I'm saying this, and give data to support it." Trust was important because what Fischer-Wright needed to do next required not only trust but also courage.

The industry of medical practice management was changing. Ten years ago, a majority of medical practices had one or two physicians. Today, that number continues to shrink, according to the American Medical

Association (AMA).[11] In a study released by AMA, the research showed many young physicians were moving away from owning practices to joining larger practices. Ownership and employment shifts may be the results of an increase in compliance costs and new payment models. In addition, health systems have been acquiring physician practices to improve patient outcomes and satisfy payment reforms. Driving this shift are the constant regulatory changes and the need to invest in technology—two issues that are driving change and the increase in private equity in many industries, not just healthcare. It should come as no surprise that to remain vital and essential, an organization must address the needs of the employer who is taking an even closer look at the return on investment of membership dues. As Fischer-Wright said, "If we stayed with an association model focused on the individual, we would not have a sustainable model. That's why we transformed."

As many medical group practices were acquired by larger healthcare institutions, the needs of both physician leaders and practice managers were rapidly changing. Fischer-Wright believed to achieve growth and retain current members, the organization needed to build a strategy to engage larger practices. Although MGMA would continue to provide the education, tools, and resources for its current membership base, it needed to look at other revenue streams to remain relevant. But it did signal a shift from being solely focused on the individual to a business model designed to support investing resources to meet the needs of where the market was headed. Fischer-Wright explained, "We looked at what members needed, and some of the products we had been providing in the past no longer met the needs of medical group practices in the future. We needed to consider the needs of the marketplace." Focusing your research primarily on your current members' needs at the exclusion of trends impacting the larger community could result in your organization becoming inessential. After all, what if your audience begins to shrink or consolidate?

MGMA experienced this firsthand when staff identified five new educational products based on research conducted with current members. Fischer-Wright asked her team to consider both the revenue the products could generate and the cost to develop programs. She wanted her team to examine the overall market potential, not merely the current level of interest. There may be a high level of interest in a topic or issue but a low or moderate opportunity to reach a larger market. As Fischer-Wright implemented the new business model for MGMA, she encouraged staff to examine all new product or program offerings to ensure a net gain could justify the investment.

By evaluating new ideas based on the strength of the business case, it became easier to say no to programs that did not align with its mission or could not produce a profit. MGMA's advocacy work and research were mission-driven activities that helped the organization stay in the forefront of issues impacting its members and customers. The new business model, however, allowed MGMA to increase its reach beyond membership. It helped the organization determine when to outsource activities, when to launch new products, and "when to kill your darlings." Many organizations have pet projects that are supported by volunteer leaders or have long been associated with the organization, even if the return on the investment has greatly diminished. By being willing to sunset some existing projects, MGMA was able to create new partnerships with vendors that could help fill a niche and provide a product or service to MGMA members and customers. "We shifted our approach to meeting the needs of the market by aggressively pursuing vendors and suppliers— two segments we would have chosen to ignore four years ago because we were focused exclusively on individual members who work within medical group practices." A driving force behind the change in who MGMA needed to serve was also the need to generate revenue so it could fund activities for its members.

With a strong commitment to staying at the forefront of changes in how healthcare is managed and delivered, MGMA began to increase its role in helping medical practices prosper by focusing on collecting and disseminating data used to make decisions. The result was the creation of new products such as industry-leading data analysis, surveys, and reports. Because in-depth research reports take time to conduct, analyze, and produce, MGMA created a tool called MGMA STAT that provides real-time answers to questions being raised by member organizations. The tool answers questions like "Should I mandate flu shots for my staff?"

and "Do other practices have cyber insurance?" With more than 4,000 individuals on the research panel, MGMA STAT asks participants a question via text. Within 48 hours, the data is aggregated, and the results and links to related articles are sent to participants. By creating a tool that can easily collect and disseminate poll data related to industry trends, MGMA not only becomes an essential partner to its members, but it also proves it provides data that matters. Such a concept is applicable even outside healthcare; members and customers seek real-time information and data, regardless of the industry or profession.

Telemedicine is an example in which MGMA leveraged an industry trend to provide value to members. Observing an increase in consumer interest in telemedicine, MGMA launched a STAT poll in January 2018 that revealed that more than 40 percent of medical groups are currently or are planning to offer telehealth services this year. In addition, MGMA conducted research, including a survey, several polls, and qualitative interviews, on the topic of telehealth to develop the MGMA Research & Analysis Report, *Telehealth: Adoption + Best Practices.* The report outlines a number of models that can help medical practices plan, implement, and operate telehealth services. It also details adoption trends, implementation challenges and tips, best practices, billing and reimbursement resources, onboarding checklists, and case studies. "Understanding the drivers of telehealth services, as well as the operating requirements, will help ensure successful adoption of these services," said Fischer-Wright. "Equally important, we must understand how healthcare consumers embrace telehealth services. Nearly two thirds of patients would like their primary care provider to offer telehealth, so we need to get better at providing these services as an industry."

As the organization began to expand its reach into new audience segments, it realized there were new opportunities to develop programs and products to better meet its needs. This led to changes in the organizational structure of its staff and who was recruited to sit on the board. The factor that perhaps had the greatest effect on the success of MGMA's new product lines, however, was the way it accelerated new ideas and embraced change. "When volunteer leaders were focused on membership, the organization would shrink. We were just looking to make people we served happy. However, when those members retire and are not replaced with new members, we need to think of new markets. When we pivoted our attention to new industries, we grew," Fischer-Wright added.

Far too often, organizations must sit on ideas until they've been fully vetted and approved by a volunteer committee or board that meets infrequently. Under Fischer-Wright's leadership, MGMA developed a business process for incubating new ideas based on markers that could more accurately forecast results—the mining of existing data. Key performance metrics, such as potential reach, matter, and they are used to green light new ideas or shift resources away from programs that are not profitable.

Once the new business model was established, Fischer-Wright needed to realign staff roles and responsibilities. The content team needed to be aligned with the business development team to ensure timely delivery of its products. The organization also created a feedback loop to develop new products and an online portal to deliver content and increase engagement. Fischer-Wright stated, "The focus on alternative markets has made the difference. We weren't being a good servant to our customers because we didn't value them relative to our members." The changes taking place at MGMA resulted in a 30 percent growth in its reach. Although membership has remained stable, the organization's customer base has grown to more than 100,000.

Fischer-Wright describes herself as having an abundance mindset. Rather than having a negative reaction to the challenges she faces, she believes that if a solution doesn't exist, she can build it—or buy it. She sees limitless possibilities and builds on what's working.

Lessons Learned From MGMA

To lead change, you need to have an abundance mindset. You need to embrace change and develop a culture that is proactive, not reactive. Fischer-Wright successfully helped MGMA transition from focusing exclusively on individual members to serving the larger community by leveraging the organization's existing relationships and rebuilding trust among its volunteer leaders. Rather than continuing to invest in efforts, activities, and ideas that no longer resonated with the marketplace, Fischer-Wright made the business case for supporting individuals and employers, as well as vendors and customers.

1. To grow your organization, don't limit your efforts to increasing membership. To achieve your mission, you may need to expand your reach and attract more customers. What does your organization currently offer—or what could it offer in the future—to meet the needs of your members' employers, customers, and vendors? What partnerships could be created that leverage your organization's strengths, reputation, and expertise and solve a problem within your marketplace?

2. Free up resources by retiring "program darlings" that no longer serve the needs of members or customers or aren't profitable. When reviewing your portfolio of benefits, do you consider the costs and expenses as well as the gross revenue?

3. Grow your customer base through new partnerships and new audience segments.

4. Adopt a business model that supports a critical evaluation of the value proposition, the cost structure, net profits, and reach.

Evolving and Disrupting

In the article "What is Disruptive Innovation?" in the December 2015 issue of the *Harvard Business Review*, Clayton M. Christensen and his co-authors describe disruption as "a process whereby a smaller company with fewer resources is able to successfully challenge established incumbent businesses." By the authors' definition, established incumbent businesses focus on the needs of certain segments to the exclusion of others. They added, "Entrants that prove disruptive begin by successfully targeting those overlooked segments, gaining a foothold by delivering more-suitable functionality—frequently at a lower price." In other words, disrupters create a market where none existed. A new entrant or competitor in the marketplace is not a disruptor if it has provided an alternative solution to an existing audience. Any organization can become a disruptor if it seeks out new audiences and meets their needs. MGMA's story of providing solutions to an underserved audience is an example of disruption. Disrupters may enter a market and provide a program, product, or service to meet a need that has

CONTINUED ON NEXT PAGE

been ignored by companies and organizations that are focused on a larger or more profitable audience. The process for changing the business strategy is an example of a pivot. There is a distinction, however, between evolving and disrupting. Not every pivot is a disruption.

In an interview, Jeff Bezos, Amazon CEO and founder, said, "What's very dangerous is not to evolve, not invent, not improve the customer experience. ... You have to have a willingness to repeatedly fail." He continued, "You do need to listen to your customers, but you also need to invent on their behalf. And it's not the customers' job to invent on their own behalf."[12] Bezos added that at Amazon, there are two ways they extend their business: they take an inventory of their existing skills and extend the business based on those strengths, and they also look at their customers' needs and acquire new skills based on that assessment. In the interview, Bezos used Amazon's Kindle to exemplify his argument of the latter—starting with the customer. The company recognized the potential market and observed that the necessary technologies for establishing a service for that market were becoming available. Bezos credited a successful holiday season in sales overall in 2010, despite the downturn economy, on the $4 billion Amazon spent on research and development over that decade. Today, Amazon dominates the e-book market in the United States, accounting for 83 percent of the e-book unit sales according to a February 2017 report from AuthorEarnings.[13]

●

CHAPTER 4

To Innovate, You Need Value

An argument is often made, using a quote commonly attributed to Henry Ford, that innovation does not come from customer input: "If I asked people what they wanted, they would have said a faster horse." However, the issue is not asking for customer input but asking the customer the wrong questions. If someone had asked, prior to the emergence of the Model T, what problem customers wanted solved, they may have complained that it took too long to get from one place to another. Asking members to rate a current experience or their interest in a current product only provides insight into their perspectives on what exists today. It does not provide the input needed to find an innovative solution to a problem.

Asking the wrong questions on program or conference evaluations is common in the association community. When a conference evaluation only measures the interest and satisfaction of those who attended, it neglects to uncover the forces that drive the decision not to attend. By developing a research strategy focused on innovation, organizations can explore the hidden reasons behind certain behaviors. By diving deeper into the challenges of non-conference attendees or nonmembers, a scientific society, for example, may learn that to provide more value, it needs to create opportunities for its audience to obtain funding and present their research. Through examining its timeline, the organization may also uncover opportunities to connect with members throughout the research cycle, not just when they are ready to present their findings. If an organization asked potential attendees questions about the last few conferences they've attended, as well as some of their interests, passions, and hobbies or what cities they love or wish to visit, the organization could learn more about the types of experiences participants are seeking and get a sense of the likelihood of a particular city drawing a larger group of convention goers.

To identify opportunities to provide more value and develop a business model that aligns value, engagement, and retention, it is essential for associations to ask questions that will guide the decision-making process, especially when it is time to make changes. For example, to measure attitudes and behaviors toward in-person events and to create personas to better target your messages, organizations should ask current members and nonmembers (both customers and lapsed members) if they feel the following sample statements accurately reflect how they feel about continuing education:

- I only participate when I am required to do so.
- I believe other methods for advancing my career/knowledge are more effective and affordable.
- I attend in-person meetings because I find them enjoyable.
- I believe conferences offer unique opportunities to develop personal contacts to benefit my career.
- I rely on the association to develop a network of contacts to address work-related issues.
- I feel in-person education is more effective than self-study or online education.
- I feel online communities are more accessible and effective in helping me build my professional network.
- I will only attend an in-person education program if my employer pays my registration fees and travel-related expenses.

- I actively contribute to online communities when they focus on specific and relevant topics.

At my company, Avenue M Group, we have crafted a series of questions that guide many of our studies into an association's value proposition.

- **What are the low, medium, and high drivers of membership and engagement?** This goes beyond areas of interest and measures the factors that influence the decision to join, register, buy, or engage. To get this point across, ask a room full of colleagues, volunteers, or friends the following: on a scale of one to five, how would you rate the importance of conducting research to find a cure for cancer? Most, if not everyone, in the room would say it is extremely important or rate it a five on a five-point scale. However, if you asked the same group of people to raise their hands if they had given money in the past 12 months to an organization conducting research to find a cure for cancer, a lot fewer would respond that they had. Measuring importance does not always tell you what motivates or drives individuals to financially support an organization—or to take any action. Individuals and organizations may believe in your association's mission and rate it as highly important to the profession or to the good of society, yet they may not join or renew their membership if other factors have more influence on their decision.

- **Is membership important or essential to the advancement of an individual's career or business success?** Across the past nine years, research conducted by Avenue M Group with more than 200,000 individuals who currently or previously maintained a membership in a professional association revealed that approximately one in four members belong to an organization primarily to support its mission and vision. This isn't to say the other three members do not support the mission. In fact, many do support the mission; however, they will not join or renew unless the organization provides a return on their investment.

- **Why do some people prefer to engage with the organization as customers? What factors into this decision?** How frequently do you survey nonmember customers? Once a year? Once a month? After every transaction? How much do you know about your nonmember customers? Are there common characteristics for this audience segment? Does your organization have a strategy for maximizing its reach with nonmembers? The decision to better understand your nonmember customers is as important as the decision to survey and analyze the demographics and behavior of current and lapsed members. Most organizations can identify a list of individuals who have made a one-time purchase and never returned. As demonstrated in the Medical Group Management Association case study in Chapter 3, it is essential for volunteer leaders and association executives to understand all the audiences they serve if they wish to expand their reach or grow membership.

- **What are the next best alternatives in the marketplace, and how do they compare to your organization's offerings?** Are the next best alternatives more affordable or accessible? Building a business model based on a unique value proposition requires understanding both the factors that drive the decision to join, engage, or consume products and services, as well as alternatives in the marketplace. If your organization's strength is that it delivers evidence-based information that requires a rigorous and time-consuming process, it may be competing with for-profit entities or other organizations that are quicker to market with information that members and others find reliable and easier to access. It's essential for organizations to examine the marketplace on a biannual or annual basis to assess how its offerings compare to those of competitors. The bottom line is that the factors an organization considers its strengths may also contribute to an erosion of users, members, and customers if next best alternatives are good enough. An organization can build a business model around being reliable, relevant, and grounded in scientific evidence, yet if the organization does not invest in or have the resources to provide digital, accessible, and affordable information, it will not be considered an indispensable resource and can experience a decline in usage and engagement.

- **What are the top challenges facing members today, and how do they affect the decision to engage with your organization and other organizations?** What issues do members expect to affect their work over the next three years? For example, a professional society serving members of a communication technology industry recently invested in uncovering trends in the profession and market. The organization understood the importance of delivering critical products and services to help its members succeed at their jobs. To better understand market demand, industry maturity, and the various issues members face, it conducted an in-depth study that explored how technology coincides with standards and regulatory development or adoption. By exploring the topics and issues by audience segment, maturity, and marketplace demand, the organization is better positioned to develop and deliver new programs, products, and services.

- **How do members search for and consume information, and does this differ by specific use?** For example, when a physician is meeting with a patient and needs to quickly search for information on a specific issue, a 300-page practice guideline or resource is unlikely to meet his or her needs. He or she may value the rigor and depth of the resource but never use it because it isn't accessible on a mobile device or it doesn't provide sufficient search capabilities. By examining how and when resources and information are used and why they are sometimes ignored, an organization can create more valuable resources and become more relevant to its members. Understanding your target audience, both its current and future needs, is essential if you wish to stay relevant and deliver on your mission.

In today's rapidly changing work environment, associations must do more than provide resources that have been thoroughly vetted through a rigorous review process that may take months or years before distribution. To be seen as innovative and, more importantly, to become a valued and essential partner to members, organizations must provide products and resources that are accessible. Doing so may require changing how associations develop, price, and distribute education and research information. While this may appear risky, maintaining the current system is its own risk. Associations want to be seen as innovative but are reluctant to commit to the changes necessary to try a new or untested approach. But in a period of continual change, remaining the same is perhaps the greater risk.

Uncharted Territory

Being first has its risks and rewards. Product and service innovation is often associated with the first company or organization to create it or widely promote it. For years, if you needed a tissue, you reached for a Kleenex; if you needed something to protect a cut, you asked for a Band-Aid. You used Scotch Tape to keep wrapping paper on a present, and the flying disc you threw to your dog was a Frisbee. All of these products, while trademarked, define the product category. However, while history is filled with stories of successful business models built around the concept of first-mover advantage, there are at least as many, if not more, stories of brands and products that improved upon the original idea and survived changing behaviors and advancements in technology. In the end, it is often the circumstances—not the strength of an existing brand, number of financial resources, or the size of an existing customer base— that determine if a product or idea will succeed or fail.

According to an April 2005 Harvard Business Review article, "The Half-Truth of First Mover Advantage," two of the main advantages to being first to market are 1) having "more time than later entrants to accumulate and master technical knowledge" and 2) establishing "an early base of customers who would find it inconvenient or costly to switch to the offerings of later entrants." Yet the authors, Fernando Suarez and Gianvito Lanzolla, also point out that the two most important factors to a company's success are not within any company's control: "the pace of technology evolution and the pace of market evolution." When the pace of change is gradual, it's difficult for new organizations to enter the space and compete with well-established brands. Kleenex, Band-Aids, Scotch Tape, and Frisbee all launched in slow-moving markets. In contrast, Google is universally recognized as the leading engine for desktop and mobile internet search, yet it entered the market after Yahoo and Infoseek. Netflix is another widely known example of a company that did not have the first-mover advantage nor the deep resources of the primary competitor, yet it was able to pivot as behaviors changed and the pace of technology accelerated. As detailed in Chapter 3, Netflix's core business didn't change; rather, it changed its delivery channel to meet changing needs and thereby capture a large share of the market.

Associations are unique in that they can take advantage of a well-established brand and a core base of members and customers yet still be nimble enough to adjust to changes in behavior, market demand, and interest. Although many associations are often slow to change their value propositions—because the risks appear to be too big or because they'd rather move into well-charted territory—the opportunities are actually far greater than in the for-profit world. Associations are bound by a mission, vision, core values, and bylaws but not by profit margins, product lines, or major investments in research and development. Their programs, products, and services support their missions, but they are not—or should not be—the foundation on which organizations are built. Your organization's mission statement is unlikely to reference a specific offering such as the annual conference or a specific publication. For-profit companies, on the other hand, are often initially built around a product line. It is why they exist—to sell products or services.

How does a 100-year-old organization become nimbler and more responsive to the needs of a changing market while still fulfilling its mission? It begins by understanding when to explore uncharted territory and when to leverage other strengths and not compete just because it is a space you've always occupied. In the book, *Seizing the White Space*, Mark W. Johnson observed that many companies can leverage their strengths and capitalize on new opportunities—as long as those opportunities fit within their well-established business model. Many businesses will, to their detriment, overlook or dismiss opportunities for growth (e.g., expanding to new customers, providing new services to existing customers) that do not seem to align with their existing strengths.[1]

When an idea appears to align well within existing resources or product lines, organizations often will invest resources and staff into developing products around the new concept. For example, continuing education has long been considered a cornerstone of the value proposition for professional and trade associations. It's no wonder, then, that when associations look to create innovative new offerings, they frequently examine opportunities to create product extensions from their existing portfolios. By doing so, however, they may miss new opportunities with new audience segments that lay adjacent to their educational programs. When a new idea with merit surfaces but does not fit neatly into current product lines, many organizations take a pass on the opportunity because it doesn't align with the existing business model of the organization. It's critical to remember that the core of any business model is the value proposition. Successful organizations must know when to adjust, change, or add to their core benefits. And, like in the case of the American Industrial Hygiene Association in Chapter 2, they must have volunteer leaders and staff who know how to adapt and pivot when the market changes.

Consider the story behind the Virgin Group, a family-owned growth capital investor. With a portfolio of more than 60 businesses serving more than 53 million customers around the world, Virgin-branded companies focus on six industries: financial services, health and wellness, music and entertainment, people and planet, telecoms and media, and travel and leisure.[2] Investing in developed and developing markets, Virgin Group identifies "opportunities in geographies or market segments where consumers are underserved" and leverages its global network and large portfolio to grow its branded companies.[3] In each sector, Virgin did not have a first-mover advantage. In fact, Virgin entered what many consider mature industries with brands that hold a strong foothold in the space. Yet Virgin was able to build a successful business by providing products and services to underserved audience segments. Virgin succeeded because it wasn't afraid to fail when venturing into new spaces while staying true to its mission and vision.

Virgin's success is based on a number of factors that are worth unpacking and examining. First, the company established a clear set of guiding principles that allowed it to invest in multiple, unrelated business lines. The common denominator in each one was the underlying idea that there may be a better way to meet the needs of the customer and delight them in ways that will build brand loyalty. Second, the company invested in areas with underserved markets and delivered a better solution to existing challenges. Founder Sir Richard Branson stated, "Virgin won't go into a new business unless they believe they can offer something that is distinct from what already exists."[4] Additionally, when asked how he has built and sustained a successful business, Branson emphasized the importance of treating his employees well, who will in turn treat their customers well. Because success rarely comes without some failures, Branson explained, "Every person, and especially every entrepreneur, should embrace failure with open arms. It is only through failure that we learn. Many of the world's finest minds have learned this the hard way."[5]

Sharing Insect Science Globally

When the March for Science was organized in 2017, its purpose was to empower a global community of science supporters, promote evidence-based policies, and help interested individuals connect with their elected officials at every level. While some critics argued that what was being advocated was based on the previous Presidential administration's agenda, others saw the March for Science as an opportunity to increase awareness around the importance of scientific funding. Interestingly, one of the most important goals to emerge from the creation of the March for Science was to help break down the barriers between scientists and their communities. Without an open dialogue about science and its impact on society, funding for research and other scientific activities may decline or cease to exist. In addition, the community recognized the importance of being held accountable for ensuring science is diverse, inclusive, and accessible to all.

Diversity, inclusion, accessibility, trust—all the essential elements to successfully achieving those goals are also critical characteristics for any organization to thrive in today's environment, regardless of the discipline. These characteristics, when embedded into the fabric of an organization's core purpose, create the value organizations seek to be relevant in the future. As such, the story about how the scientific community is raising its profile and connecting with its community is relevant to any organization.

One of the first professional associations to publicly support the March for Science was the Entomological Society of America (ESA). Founded in

1889, ESA is the largest organization in the world serving the professional and scientific needs of entomologists and individuals in related disciplines. And while the organization has long been established as the voice of the profession, it recognized the need to expand its focus and help scientists communicate the importance of taking lessons learned in the lab to a broader audience. Taking a bold stand in support of the research and work being done by its members and others within the scientific community is a priority for ESA, and it is one component of its value proposition.

ESA Executive Director David Gammel, FASAE, CAE, said, "Our value proposition isn't one thing; it's the sum of many actions we are taking to ensure our members can exchange scientific information, contribute to the field of insect science, and advance their careers." While many organizations focus on creating a strong value proposition, he understands that it is equally important to deliver an exceptional experience.

Acknowledging that the single biggest issue facing the scientific profession is the funding environment, ESA understood it needed to take a leadership role in that discussion to deliver value to its members. Gammel explained, "We have a belief in science and investing in it. It can take nine to 12 years to train a new scientist, going from undergraduate through a post-doc position. When it comes to research, you can't pivot on a dime, so sustained high levels of funding for science is important. A lot of researchers work in the federal government. If there is a shutdown, they can't go into their labs. If their experiment is based on a season of year, if they shutdown, they miss their window, even if the shutdown is only for one week." With a renewed sense of urgency, ESA has become more strategic in its approach to addressing the problems its members are facing.

While ESA has been serving the scientific community for more than a century, when Gammel arrived in 2011, the organization was at a pivotal moment in its history. After going through a financial crisis and restructuring process, ESA emerged on solid footing and was well positioned to deliver a different value proposition to its members. "When I arrived at ESA, I didn't have a grand strategy to transform them, but I looked at how we could improve everything," Gammel stated. "I looked at how we could improve the value of our meeting and how we could improve the value for our early career professionals. Where is there energy and desire to engage new members? And I hired staff that were passionate about creating a fantastic member experience."

ESA made significant investments in its marketing technology and staff, but leadership recognized that marketing efforts wouldn't be able to create sustained returns on their own; ESA needed to create an exceptional experience. Similar to many other professional societies, ESA serves a mature market. From its annual conference to its internationally acclaimed journals and *American Entomologist* periodical, ESA is the premier organization for researchers, teachers, students, consultants, and others interested in the discipline. Yet engagement and a sense of connectedness were not as strong for the rank-and-file members, and it appeared to be missing from the next generation of scientists. Its meeting lacked energy and excitement. It often looked backward rather than to the future. For example, the opening plenary was often dry and featured keynotes lauding the historical accomplishments of entomologists; they rarely focused on the future of the profession. ESA now opens the meeting with a keynote that speaks about the future, and this small change altered the dynamic and set the stage for a meeting focused on what's ahead for the discipline.

ESA also invested time and resources into better understanding the factors that impact meeting attendance. Gammel understood that his members work in academia, so presenting at a scientific conference is important to their careers. "That's a driver for us. At the individual and personal level, we help members build their CV [curriculum vitae]," he said. To increase interest and attendance at the meeting, ESA developed a strategy to increase submissions to present at the Annual Conference. As Gammel helped guide the organization by creating a more meaningful and relevant experience at its meeting, attendance grew. "If you look at the numbers, the growth over the past five years has been dramatic for a mature market. It had a synergistic effect." When Gammel first joined ESA in 2011, the Annual Conference attracted approximately 2,700 attendees. By 2017, around 3,600 people attended—a roughly 33 percent growth over seven years for a mature profession and meeting.

Next, ESA selected more attractive cities for its meeting. "We were in second-tier and third-tier cities. While these cities may offer more affordable hotels and meeting space, we know people wouldn't go out of their way to attend the meeting there. Although the quality of the meeting is the first driver, having a meeting in a fun and exciting city is important. We contracted with cities that were growing, on the hip side of things." In an effort to improve all aspects of its conference, ESA looked at cities that offered attractive experiences for young people. Gammel explained, "We were able to do this by offering multiyear dates and looking ahead 10 to 12 years. Cities that may not have been interested in our meeting in the past, due to our size or other factors, were submitting bids. Improving the location of our conference helped increase attendance."

Finally, Gammel recognized the need to build a pipeline from the student community—the future of the organization. ESA offers students meaningful development through a large student competition that takes place during two days of the conference and through many opportunities to volunteer in the meeting, including developing symposia and workshops. Students can present research, be judged, receive feedback, and be eligible for awards. By creating a value proposition unique to students, ESA is planting the seeds for long-term relationships with a key audience segment.

ESA subsidizes its students and loses money on them, but the organization sees it as an investment. The balance it needed to strike was to make the focus on students sustainable by converting them into full members when they progress in their careers. "If you can change the conversion rate, you will see growth," said Gammel. To accomplish this, ESA began to reach out to entomology departments at educational institutions to find ways to support student participation between when they are doing research and when they are ready to present. It also opened up roles for students, so they could serve on committees. Gammel said, "It's lots of little things we do so that we don't lose people. Students will eventually turn into meeting attendees and members and scientists who will publish with us. It's about building a lifecycle and providing value at every stage."

Another area where ESA is investing resources to increase the value proposition and help members achieve their goals is helping members better communicate the importance of their work to policymakers, influencers, and decision makers. "ESA offers tools, resources, and programs to help members better communicate. They now understand it because of the current funding environment. The general public doesn't always understand the impact of their work, so scientists need to talk to people about their work," Gammel said. ESA also offers sessions at its annual conference on how to communicate with nonscientists.

The Importance of Creating a Welcoming Experience

The most frequently asked question by volunteer leaders and staff is, "What can we offer that would provide enough value to encourage nonmembers to join and current members to renew?" To answer this question, your organization should evaluate its benefits and measure their effect on the overall satisfaction with the association. In many ways, access, affordability, and personal relevance drive the decision to join and engage. Experience also matters. Whether it is the ease of making the transaction, ease of accessing the information, or the environment of a conference or event, experience matters. What is the right balance? For the Entomological Society of America (ESA), it is helping its members succeed professionally and increasing awareness of both the profession and the need to support science-based initiatives. It is also about creating an experience like none other.

While creating opportunities and cultivating engaging experiences are important, they will not provide the connections you are seeking with new and evolving audiences if the environment is not safe, hospitable, and productive for everyone. Although ESA clearly pivoted its approach to creating and delivering an exceptional and valued meeting experience, Executive Director David Gammel is quick to point out the importance of developing a code of conduct for its meetings. "We enforce a message that we won't put up with bad behavior—our meeting is a safe place. We have gender neutral bathrooms. We offer child care support, so people with young families can participate. We help offset child care costs. We recognize the young scientists. We want to help them participate in our meeting. We have mothers' rooms." Gammel frequently reviews ways to make the experience more inclusive and welcoming, adding, "Anytime I see an opportunity to make our meeting easier to attend, I want to do it."

Although some may not look at the improvements to the conference as being a pivotal business decision, for a traditional scientific society whose core strength and benefit is rooted in this effort, it is substantial. Gammel explained, "Years ago, the conference had the look and feel of a business meeting. We celebrated achievements of the past. While it is important to recognize where we've been, there is a better time and place for that acknowledgement. We now open the meeting on where the discipline is going, and this is what you need to know to go on that ride."

Lessons Learned From ESA

1. See your organization from the viewpoint of a member. Before you build a better value proposition, you need to understand how that is defined from the member's perspective. This begins with an in-depth understanding of the individuals or companies serving the profession.

   a. Where do they see themselves—or if they manage their own companies, where do they see their businesses—in three, five, and seven years?

   b. What do they need to achieve their goals? For example, do they need better communication skills or an advocate to ensure government regulations are favorable? Do they need management or leadership training?

   c. What barriers prevent them from engaging or participating with the organization? When looking at the entire lifecycle of a member, would an investment in members during the beginning of their careers increase the likelihood of creating lifelong connections throughout their careers? Could the organization subsidize their memberships and participation in this early career stage? Where could the organization increase market share and revenue?

   d. What external issues (e.g., government funding, travel restrictions) might impact their ability to practice and fulfill their professional obligations? What is the best way to help members overcome these challenges? Are they local, state, national, or global challenges?

2. Improve your value proposition by creating better experiences. Content matters, but so does the experience organizations deliver. For ESA, the

experience begins with increasing the ease, awareness, and opportunities to submit research to present at its annual conference. Recognizing its role as a CV builder, ESA understood that to thrive in the future, it needed a business model that encouraged, supported, and subsidized engagement among students and early career scientists. In addition, by focusing on and improving all aspects of the annual conference experience, ESA was able to significantly increase attendance.

3. Invest money and resources in activities that will increase diversity and ensure inclusion. Redesigning its conference to be more forward-looking, from choosing its keynote speaker to selecting progressive and lively cities, helped ESA emerge as a leader in the field. By expanding opportunities to individuals at all stages of their careers and ensuring members have the support they need to attend the conference, ESA did more than create a policy—it created a more productive environment.

4. Create an environment that encourages and supports change. The riskier move is to stand still while the world changes around you. Gammel and his team changed nearly everything about its flagship offering, the Annual Conference. If he had asked his members to rate the experience of attending the meeting in the past and if they had expressed moderate to high levels of satisfaction, it would have been easy for the board and volunteer leaders to push back on any changes to the format, speakers, location, and program content. Instead, ESA's leadership recognized that to stay ahead, they couldn't be complacent.

What Kept You Moving Forward May Now Hold You Back
Most individuals look for solutions to the challenges they are facing *right now.* For some, it is finding new clients or growing their businesses while others hope to advance their careers, improve the care of patients, or solve a problem through science and engineering. In many industries, workers struggle to find enough hours in the day to complete the tasks they are required to do and stay current on trends. Regardless of the profession or industry, what matters for many is if your organization can provide a solution to what is holding them back from achieving their goals.

The challenge many organizations face is the fear that a change to their business models may result in a heavy financial loss. The basic architecture supporting many associations includes four major revenue streams: membership dues, continuing education registrations, product sales, and advertising/sponsorships. Changing one of the four elements could have an immediate effect on an organization if it has not already identified a reliable, major new source of revenue. This situation often prevents organizations from venturing into new spaces that could provide more value to the changing needs of current and future members. For example, many associations rely heavily on the revenue generated from their annual conferences. For some, it may account for up to a third or more of the total operating budget. Although the meeting may be highly rated by the members who attend each year, if that audience is shrinking due to a retiring member base or widespread budget cuts in the field, the meeting should be assessed for how well it can continue to meet the needs or solve the problems of those in the profession. Without an honest assessment of whether an association's offerings are meeting the needs of members and customers, the door is left open for competitors or new organizations to fill the gap.

To illustrate, in *The Art of Membership,* I share the story of how SurePayroll successfully entered a mature and crowded market by providing a better solution than its larger, well-established competitors. Similar to today's members who want a better solution to get the job done, SurePayroll understood that small business owners needed an affordable, convenient, and easy way to process payroll. Existing solutions did not offer the combination of all three qualities. The major payroll companies had built a business model on an infrastructure that included dozens, if not hundreds, of processing centers and included large staffs, printed checks, and delivery people—all of the costs they then had to factor into the price. SurePayroll created a solution that essentially allowed it to more easily implement enhancements and keep up with the demands of its customers.

This story is one of thousands that can be told about how a new company or organization can enter a market and compete against a well-known brand with a large market share if it provides an affordable, convenient solution based on the needs of the *customer,* not the needs of the providing organization. Even if your association is not at risk of being replaced, its programs, products, and services may become outdated and no longer relevant if your organization does not innovate. Does your organization reassess its portfolio to ensure it is delivering the solutions in an affordable, convenient manner? It's a question executives and board members should consider when reviewing their budgets, strategic plans, and product lines. The value of your organization will be reassessed by your members, prospects, customers, and partners every time they turn to your organization for a solution.

The Real Risk is Stagnation

When Christine McEntee, MHA, FASAE, arrived at the American Geophysical Union (AGU) in 2010, the organization was well established as the preeminent international force for the promotion of geophysical endeavors. Its 60,000 members helped develop solutions for the sustainability of the planet. From rainfall rates to earthquake probabilities, the study and understanding of Earth and space are essential to the long-term health and well-being of all. And while AGU and its members focused on a variety of trends impacting Earth science and space, a number of challenges began to surface, including an increased politicization of science, a decline in federal funding, an increased need to preserve Earth's resources, and a growth of inter-, multi-, and transdisciplinary science. In addition, AGU recognized a growing need to improve members' abilities to communicate science to nonscientists.

To address these challenges, McEntee explored ways to transform AGU's business operations. "It wasn't a turnaround situation. We had energy to drive change. We knew we wanted to go from good to great," McEntee shared. She began a conversation with the organization's leadership by asking them, "What do you want to say your story is, and how will we get there?"

Adding to a list of concerns, the organization's leaders recognized the trend toward open access publications, which could dramatically alter AGU's primary revenue stream and dilute its value proposition. In addition, the operational processes and technologies that supported

AGU publications were outdated. This led to a historic decision from the board to move from self-publishing to a publishing partnership. "It shored up our revenue and gave us a chance to partner with a company that focused on scholarly publishing," McEntee explained. AGU transitioned sales, copy editing, production, and the publishing technology platform to Wiley. In addition, AGU brought in an experienced publishing professional who is a Ph.D. scientist to lead the transition into a future of open science being fueled by the digital age and the age of big data in science. By improving AGU's operational business model, the organization's output has grown 10 percent per year, and it was able to launch three new journals after a drought of more than 10 years without a new publication. The move also helped the organization shorten the time from accepted manuscript to publication, helping it stay on the leading edge of data sharing. And while the move was clearly the right one to take, at the time it required eliminating 80 staff positions.

Once the organization transitioned its publication operations to Wiley, it transformed its weekly print newspaper into a daily, online, freely available Earth and space science news site. In years past, AGU distributed a printed newsletter with small 9-point type. "We needed to embrace 21st century media platforms," McEntee said. AGU also took a leadership role in advancing open sharing of the underlying data that supports research. AGU was awarded a $1 million grant from the Arnold Foundation to bring together research institutions, publishers, funders, and data repositories to work with data informatics, creating data standards, data curation, and quality control so that the underlying data could be open and reproducible to further research.

While the organization had established itself as a leader for scientific innovation, rigor, and interdisciplinary focus, internally, its approach to communicating with nonscientists and policymakers could be described as traditional and outdated. Breaking away from AGU's traditional approach to sharing information, data, and news, the organization needed to change how it developed relationships with policymakers and influencers in Washington, DC. "We had to build and expand our in-house capabilities if we wanted to have an enhanced presence on Capitol Hill and with the administration," said McEntee. Although AGU routinely shared information, it found it difficult to have its voice heard during important news cycles and when key decisions were being made in Congress. McEntee changed how the association communicated with key influencers by linking public affairs, media relations, and grassroots engagement (including training and support for AGU members), which enabled a team-based approach for routinely sharing information directly and indirectly with policymakers through traditional and nontraditional media sources. And by many accounts, these efforts appear to be having an impact. AGU fostered the establishment of an Earth and science caucus in the House of Representatives, and its members are requesting to participate in the political process both at home and by flying into Washington, DC. "In the last two years, we are getting calls from congressional offices and had questions inserted into issues related to climate change. People are starting to call us when issues arise regarding Earth science and space," McEntee stated.

Once AGU raised its profile outside the scientific community, McEntee began the work needed to update its membership operations. Although the organization has more than 60,000 members in 137 countries, it did not manage its own membership system. Instead, AGU was part of a federation and used its services to issue member renewals and collect revenue. Recognizing an opportunity to modernize its systems, mine its data, and transform the way it customizes its communication, the organization transitioned to an internal system that would enable it to increase engagement and enhance a feeling of connectedness among the community.

McEntee cited AGU's investment in new initiatives as part of the reason the association has accomplished so much. "The board gives us up to 4 percent of our investment earnings to use for strategic initiatives. So, for the past five years, we've been investing a total of $4 million a year to build new services and new programs. And it's below the budget line." Further, the organization follows both a strategic plan for long-range planning and a multiyear plan that is updated annually.

To ensure AGU stays at the forefront of the profession and is considered relevant and essential to policymakers who make decisions that impact AGU's members, McEntee and her team monitor what is happening outside of the profession—in higher education, digital and social media, artificial intelligence, political trends, and other areas. And while McEntee has helped AGU expand its presence, increase its relevancy, and improve communication to internal and external audiences, she recognizes work still needs to be done to ensure a higher level of diversity and inclusion. AGU's commitment to diversity and inclusion begins with a statement in its strategic plan that addresses the need to use its position to build the global talent pool in Earth and space science. McEntee said, "We still have a lot of Western thinking, but we are committed to expanding engagement from individuals outside the United States." Early career professionals and students serve on all committees and task forces and are represented on the board and council as full participants. She added, "We also just approved a new affiliation and engagement model for the organization. We are trying to go from a formal structure to enabling a network of connections."

One area where McEntee believes it is important for the organization to take a leadership role is addressing the issue of sexual harassment in the sciences. "Our policy says it's actual scientific misconduct, not just inappropriate behavior. We are hosting town halls and workshops, and we were asked to testify on Capitol Hill about it." These efforts demonstrate a business model based on providing value, access, and a sense of connectedness to both the scientific community and the general public.

McEntee gives credit to AGU's board and its staff for leading the transition and change. And this may be one of the most important components that has led to the successes the organization has achieved over the years: Only individuals who agree to act collectively for the betterment of the organization may serve. There is no place at the table for someone who wishes to act on behalf of a segment of the audience.

As AGU prepares for its centennial celebration in 2019, it recognizes that adapting to future trends does not mean the previous direction was wrong or uninformed. An organization can acknowledge the value of its past direction and leadership while arguing for a new approach in the future. "We will look at our rich history and what we've accomplished and then pivot to where the future is heading. It's an exciting time," McEntee said. "We live and breathe our strategic plan and values. Every agenda item is tied to it. It's not always perfect every time, but we have a lot to be proud of. It is truly a partnership between staff and members. It's more important to have the right people in the room than worrying about who makes the decision."

AGU is not afraid to take risks. "You try things, and if they don't work, you fix it, and that is what we do at AGU. If we don't try things, we are not innovating. But we have to be allowed to make mistakes," she said. AGU recognizes that as a scientific society, it must operate within a new business model that is sustainable, transparent, and inclusive in ways that are responsive to members and stakeholders. Part of the way AGU achieves this is by enhancing current revenue sources while also expanding beyond its existing revenue model of publications and meetings.

Lessons Learned From AGU

1. Plan for a pivot even when your organization is at a peak in its popularity. When AGU began its transformation eight years ago, it was not in a turnaround situation. It could have stayed the course, as this is often viewed as the less risky move when there isn't a financial incentive to change or when there isn't a steady decline in membership. However, organizations should not wait until they've experienced a decline to consider changes to their business models. In fact, many of the most successful business ventures and nonprofit organizations pivoted during the peak of their popularity. Even today, as it gets ready to celebrate its centennial year and has launched and reinvented many of its offerings, AGU is considering its next pivot and paying close attention to trends to ensure it remains relevant.

2. When venturing into new spaces, don't be afraid to realign personnel and financial resources. The opportunity cost of staying with a traditional business model—in AGU's case, its in-house publishing department—can create a barrier to progress. Today, nearly all new ventures require an investment in technology and digital platforms. As organizations identify new sources of revenue and new approaches to informing and engaging their communities, it will require making

changes that may result in a reorganization of staff and the development of new partnerships.

3. Build a partnership between your organization's executive staff and its volunteer leadership that is built on trust and respect. AGU's board supports new ideas by giving a percentage of investment income to help fund new initiatives. This show of respect and trust make staff more willing to take chances and innovate, even at the risk of failure.

4. Develop a business model designed for sustainability by looking outside your community to identify trends and build relationships. In today's global economy, one sector's trends are likely to affect every sector. From technology and open access to communication and continuing education, attitudes and behaviors are rapidly changing, and associations need to adapt with them.

Start With Value

Long before I joined the association community, I was a photojournalist for a daily metropolitan newspaper. During a typical seven and half hour shift, my assignments ran the gamut from taking a portrait of a World War II veteran for a story about Pearl Harbor to covering a high school football game. In fact, most days, I had to cover four to five assignments and leave enough time to develop, edit, and print the photos in the darkroom. Among the items in my camera bag, I usually carried three lenses: a wide-angle lens, a portrait lens, and a longer telephoto lens. Each one served a purpose, helping me tell a story by standing closer or farther away from my subjects. On each assignment, I needed to consider the most appropriate lens based on a variety of conditions.

Similar to choosing the right lens to cover a news assignment, before you can redesign or modify your business model, you must consider the value proposition from the perspective of different audience segments, looking at your organization through a number of different lenses.

A Tale of Two Cities

With an abundance of locally sourced food and drinks from award-winning eateries as well as unassuming cafes, Des Moines, Iowa, may surprise foodies and vegetarians alike. The city offers a sophisticated vibe at an affordable and accessible price. It has more than 13,000 hotel rooms and direct flights from 22 destinations. And vacationers and meeting attendees will find a variety of activities, shopping, attractions, and events.[6] Atlanta, by contrast, offers more than 90,000 hotel rooms; world-class attractions, including the Georgia Aquarium, World of Coca-Cola, Centennial Olympic Park, and CNN Worldwide; and an airport that provides direct, nonstop access from more than 150 U.S. cities and 75 international destinations.[7] Its compact, walkable convention and entertainment district, endless dining choices, and numerous nightlife spots create a very different experience from the smaller midwestern city of Des Moines. Both destinations must attract visitors and meetings to their cities, yet their convention and visitors bureaus have vastly different budgets and resources to accomplish this task.

Before Don Welsh took over as CEO of Destinations International (formerly Destination Marketing Association International), the organization struggled to articulate its value proposition, in part because of the vast range of audience segments it served. Although organizations with annual operating budgets of less than $500,000 have different needs than organizations with budgets exceeding $100 million, Destinations International looked at them through the same lens and did not differentiate its solutions based on the audience segment. "What you need in Iowa is not what you need in Atlanta. We needed to consider the budgets of our members and provide resources and solutions based on their different needs," said Welsh.

Soon after joining the organization in 2016, Welsh went on a listening tour to find out what members wanted, needed, and most importantly, were willing to support financially. Welsh recalled, "It was a very painful listening tour to realize we were very misaligned. It created an opportunity for our competitors to step in. I quickly realized we needed to align our value proposition with what was needed for our members."

This led to the realization that the organization really only had one primary objective: "We exist to make our members more successful." At the beginning of the restructuring process, Destinations International established four core pillars under which it would deliver value—community, advocacy, education, and networking.

"Nearly everything needed to be changed when I arrived," Welsh shared. The organization launched a new name to reflect the broader audience it serves, a brand strategy to increase awareness, and a new website in 2017. Once the foundation for the organization had been established, Welsh and his team identified a number of major and minor initiatives that could provide immediate value to their members and help member organizations attract more visitors to their destinations. Destinations International launched the online Member Forum, produced 11 professional development summits and learning opportunities in addition to its Annual Convention, held its first Advocacy Summit, and reimagined Destination Showcase, its premier event.

Because knowledge and data can help fuel growth for its members, the association updated and expanded its research products and destination tools, including a new Event Impact Calculator and the DestinationNEXT Futures Study on key trends in the tourism industry. Welsh said, "When we develop products, like our event calculator or other reports, we used to focus just on serving the U.S. market. We've begun increasing our efforts to expand our reach and monetize our products in destinations we never thought of going to in the past. The products and services that bear our name will become the global standard for the industry. When organizations need to measure the value of the meetings held in their cities, they will turn to us."

The current political environment is an important factor in Destinations International's increased focus on advocacy. "There has never been a time when U.S. tourism has been under attack like it is now. There is an effort to minimize the government. We've had to work with our members, be their third-party advocate to support what they do." He added, "With the significant reductions in funding, our members need us to talk about the value proposition of destination organizations."

The next challenge for Welsh and his team is to ensure current and prospective members become aware of and understand the wealth of resources available to them through the organization. He explained, "Many of the members who are benefiting from what we are doing don't know what we've done. Many destination CEOs don't know how many products or services or events their team is going to. We need to articulate our value because now, we are worthy of the investment."

Once the value proposition was created, Destinations International needed to align its membership dues structure to ensure it had a sustainable business plan for the future. The goals of the new business model included shifting the emphasis of revenue from event registrations to membership dues. The new model had to offer more equitable membership levels based on budget categories while creating value at every level. It also needed to provide an easy entry point for smaller organizations to join.

Prior to changing the dues model, the leap in dues increases per budget size ranged from 17 percent to 181 percent. In other words, although membership dues were based on an organization's annual operating budget, some organizations were paying a significantly higher percentage of their budget in dues. After a deeper examination of how many members existed within each tier, Destinations International recognized an opportunity to increase the number of budget categories to better align resource usage with the size of the organization. By the end of the dues restructuring process, it was able to simplify the dues structure for member organizations with budgets less than $2 million and expand the number of categories for members with significantly larger annual operating budgets.

The next step in synchronizing value and cost was examining the total spend on events, products, education, and sponsorships. By mining the data, Avenue M Group was able to help Destinations International determine the types of programs, products, and services being purchased or used based on budget size. This step became one of the most important ones in the process. It helped inform the decision regarding what benefits to bundle with membership, how to promote membership based on the size of the organization, and how best to engage members to ensure they will renew the following year. This step reinforced the perception that what was needed, valued, and used by a member organization in Iowa was vastly different from the benefits needed by a larger destination such as Atlanta.

Once you fully understand the various needs of members based on their size, budget, and what they need to be successful, you can design a membership model that aligns value and cost. "I think when you are in a situation of survival and when you inherit an organization that is upside down, it's important to keep an eye on current operations and rapidly move forward with the changes needed to thrive in the future. We had to fix the plane while it was still in the air," Welsh stated. To be successful, "you need to make sure you have the right people for the right job." The result was a more equitable dues structure that provided a strong value proposition and made it easier to justify a dues increase to organizations that fell into the highest paying tier of membership.

Identifying the problem and the possible solutions is step one. Aligning the value with what people are willing to pay is equally important. The greater the challenge or problem and the more your audience believes your products and programs provide real solutions, the more likely they will invest (that is, join, support, and engage) with your organization.

The Role of Employers

Innovation and public accounting are not frequently grouped together in the same sentence—unless you are the Ohio Society of Certified Public Accountants (OSCPA). Although the more common definition of innovation is a new idea, method, or device, it can also be defined as the introduction of new value. And that is how one could describe OSCPA and its approach to delivering valuable resources to its members. As the hub of knowledge, learning, and advocacy for CPAs and accounting professionals, OSCPA has more than 100 years of experience helping to build stronger communities across Ohio. Representing 85,000 CPAs and accounting professionals, OSCPA has embraced its role of helping to grow and diversify Ohio's future accounting workforce. And while continuing education has long been a key component of OSCPA's value proposition, the organization's leadership identified an opportunity to empower its members to drive value as trusted and strategic business advisors.

When Scott Wiley, FASAE, CAE, joined the organization as its CEO in 2013, he did not find an organization in need of a turnaround strategy. It had long been active and successful in advancing public policy and providing high-quality continuing education to Ohio CPAs. "Historically, OSCPA had been very active in public policy," said Wiley. "We were the only accounting association that endorsed candidates at the state and federal level. And our second largest revenue was from continuing education. In that space, OSCPA had really innovated in how they delivered continuing education to accounting professionals." The rapid pace of advancements in technology is one of the driving forces behind the disruptive continuing education movement. From massive open online courses to the growth in usage of video and podcasts, the demand for mobile learning opportunities delivered in smaller, bite-sized chunks has increased. OSCPA was the first state CPA society to use on-demand webinars to reach its members and customers, and it led the way for CPA societies to provide 10-minute, fully credited learning modules called Quick Bytes. Making the transition to microlearning was essential as the demographics of OSCPA's membership shifted to include younger genera-tions in the workforce. Although OSCPA's Quick Byte series is meeting the needs of today's members, Wiley recognized that the organization cannot rest on the success of this program; what had been important in the past was not all that was needed to ensure the organization remained relevant in the future.

While OSCPA enjoys a high level of brand loyalty from many of its members, Wiley does not believe this alone ensures a strong future. "What we've always been, while valuable, is less relevant to who we connect with in the business world. There is a view that the OSCPA just provided free or low-priced continuing professional education to the market. This perception will not sustain us," he said. For all of its efforts to innovate and adapt to the changing behaviors of its members, the associa-tion began to see a decline in engagement. The organization had kept its eye on the changing needs of its members but now realized the impor-tance of expanding its reach. "When we looked at what strengthened our brand in the past (discounts on education and information to keep members up to date) and we examined the indicators that drive member-ship growth, it became clear that we needed to focus on new audiences and new benefits." A generation was retiring, and younger members were less inclined to join the professional society. Although a dues increase could cover a decrease in revenue, Wiley firmly believed this wasn't the solution the organization needed to remain relevant. In fact, OSCPA implemented a freeze on dues during a time of transition. OSCPA needed to establish a strong connection to the future of the profession.

Although OSCPA had a deteriorating member base, the market was not shrinking. It became clear that the organization needed to shift its focus from a member orientation to a market orientation. To pivot and redefine OSCPA's business model, Wiley needed to explore new audiences and a new process for assessing its value, a substantially different approach from what the organization had done in the past. The old model offered news, content, educational opportunities, and a sense of belonging in exchange for a flat membership fee. In this model, OSCPA owned and sold content and education to Ohio CPAs. Wiley shared, "In a sense, we are a retail operation. But the retail business model is under assault. If we tinker with it, we could be a member-oriented knowledge organization. We needed to shift from retail to becoming the knowledge source for our members and the field. Knowledge is fluid. No one owns it." The goal of the new approach was to increase the CPA's sphere of influence. "Because we had credibility in the marketplace, we were able to thrive. Our core asset in a market is our members—their know-how and experience. And that can be developed for any partner, not just members." By leveraging the knowledge and experience of CPAs in a new way, OSCPA could help its members advance into the role of trusted business advisor. And by making the shift from member orientation to this open market, it could introduce to the larger business market what the CPA profession has to offer.

Accounting firms are gaining a stronger presence in the middle market (i.e., the companies that account for the middle third of the U.S. economy's revenue), a place they had not been in the past. Wiley observed that the biggest area of growth for accounting firms may be through their consulting practices and that many individuals who work in areas under the accounting umbrella may not be CPAs. OSCPA needed to move quickly to understand where the mid-market was going and what issues or challenges were faced there.

OSCPA began looking at accounting firm leadership and asking questions about what concerned them most or what kept them up at night. "We don't focus on mass marketing and email; we pick up the phone and get more personal. Our new approach is to come to you and understand you and develop solutions that meet your needs," Wiley added. This would allow the association to be relevant, valuable, and more responsive to the market. Wiley understood that solutions were needed to meet the needs of employers, rather than programs and products to sell to the current base. This required a pivot in OSCPA's business model, as well as a shift in mentality for OSCPA's leaders. It's similar to the analogy given by Harvard Business School professor Theodore Levitt: People don't go to the hardware store to buy a drill; they go to buy a hole.[8]

One concern appeared to be shared by nearly every firm Wiley visited. What kept the firm management up at night was their struggle with succession planning. Managing partners identified a lack of soft skills among the staff who had the professional experience to move ahead but did not know how to manage and lead a team. What he heard from the firm leaders struck a cord and pointed to an opportunity to fill a gap within the workplace. Wiley said, "We want to help firms develop their talent and encourage them to stay in the field. OSCPA is putting more of our energy into efforts to help firms create their future." By providing coaching and staff development, OSCPA could help both CPAs and their employers succeed—a simple concept that would take a multiyear investment of time and resources.

Four years after joining OSCPA, Wiley looks back and firmly states that business model innovation or transformation is not for the faint of heart. It takes moral courage because you are disrupting an existing culture, and sometimes that culture has very strong roots. "You are changing the essence of work and how we think about work," he said. For example, members from solo and small practices traditionally formed the core membership within the organization. When Wiley saw a market for this group deteriorating while other markets were growing, he recognized the need to shift internal resources. "Our solo firms have been our bread and butter, but it is a dying group. So how much do we continue to meet their needs? If they don't have updated technology, do we still try to meet their needs? I'd say no. We need to focus on where the market is emerging. For us, it is the middle market and the emerging economy." This required OSCPA to find other ways to support some audiences without dedicating resources to develop new product lines for them. "We serve as a conduit for them to get other resources. It might be someone else's core business, and we can create a partnership so that they have access to those resources." Wiley believes that to move forward, the organization also had to stop providing benefits in areas that no longer served the larger audience. He added, "The best thing we did was stop doing many things. Leaders need to know that comes with pain and strife. That is significant. There is nothing that suggests to me that we won't be in a continuous change state." Even when implementing changes, he recognized that the organization always needs to be prepared to pivot again to adapt to the market.

Wiley spoke to the important role of an organization's leaders when he described the challenges of successfully navigating a rapidly changing environment. As the CEO, it is important for him to be externally oriented yet connected to the staff so that they can act on the changes he wishes to implement. Fortunately for OSCPA, its board fully embraced the changes he has lead. Because the board members are trusted business advisors, they can easily rise to the role of helping guide the organization forward. OSCPA's board has four lines of sight: oversight, insight, strategic foresight, and hindsight. Although most boards function in a similar way, OSCPA's board spends the majority of its time providing insight and strategic foresight because the organization has the systems and processes in place to ensure it is operating at a high level. OSCPA's board is engaged in making decisions that impact the strategic direction of the organization.

According to Wiley, you also need the right team with the right focus to effectively transform an organization. Once he had the board focused on the strategy and vision, he re-examined how he managed his internal team. He found that he was spending a significant amount of time every month in the traditional one-on-one meetings and smaller group discussions with key employees and teams to hear what they were seeing and offer feedback—important but time consuming. Wiley repositioned the staff going from eight direct reports to three; this allowed him to get more time back in his day to focus on the tasks he was uniquely qualified to do for the organization: business development and growth. He explained, "I am out much more. I count on our senior leadership team to have functional responsibility and have equal responsibility for enterprise management. It requires them to perform at a higher level." Wiley added, "Now on a monthly basis and a quarterly basis, I sit down with key leadership and others to review our business. It allows us to monitor and manage our business closely in real time and make adjustments and tweaks as needed. It makes us much nimbler." On a monthly and quarterly basis as OSCPA checks its progress, it can evaluate quickly and pivot if necessary to stay ahead of the curve.

Finally, Wiley noted how critical it was to find and bring in people with a diversity of perspectives and backgrounds. "While we still have folks with association competencies and skills, we hired some individuals directly from our market who don't have an association background. It's invaluable to us. They are bringing for-profit business transformation. It helps us understand how the market thinks about these issues." He added, "OSCPA understands the importance of being able to connect with members, prospects, influencers, and others in a language that resonates within the community. We will still be in the place of business transformation, even if we are not in a continuous change state." At its core, OSCPA remains focused on providing exceptional learning experiences, an inclusive welcoming community, and tools and resources for its members and customers, as well as serving as the voice for Ohio's CPAs and the accounting profession. This hasn't changed. What has changed is what they are delivering and to whom.

Lessons Learned From OSCPA

1. Ensure you have clarity on who your association serves. Do you serve the members or the profession? Are you a member-driven organization or do you focus on how to move the profession forward and stay relevant? If you serve the profession, you may need to expand the scope of the audiences you serve to achieve your mission. You may not need to be a traditional individual membership organization in the

future—instead, you may be an association that serves many different audiences, including members, employers, legislators, media, the public, and others.

2. If your current focus limits your ability to reach a broader market, change it. Regardless of whether your organization is caused-based (e.g., women's health or advancing engineering knowledge) or focused on the individuals who work in the profession (e.g., physicians, CPAs, small business owners), most organizations would benefit from expanding their reach. Recognizing that nearly all jobs or positions within a profession are connected to each other is an important first step in broadening an organization's reach and providing more value.

3. When looking for new opportunities to provide value, ask potential members and decision makers to describe the biggest frustrations and challenges they regularly face. Dig deeper to understand why they believe the challenge exists and what kind of influence you can have if you were able to offer a solution. Don't ask potential members or decision makers to solve the problem. That's your job. Organizations need to examine, at a deeper level, what problems need solving and why the problems exist. While surveys are a useful tool, personal conversations are sometimes better at uncovering the why behind the what. Many new CEOs will go on a listening tour after they join an organization and before they institute changes to the value proposition, structure, or business model. In the future, a listening tour should be conducted annually if an organization wishes to stay relevant and understand the real issues or challenges their members, customers, and others within the profession face on a daily basis. Identifying new opportunities to create value begins by listening to the individuals on the front lines of the profession.

   a. Identify and meet with audience segments beyond your traditional member base. This may include supervisors, colleagues in other departments or work settings, support staff, customer service or front-line staff, and referral sources.

b. Within your membership, have discussions with individuals regarding the challenges faced by groups underrepresented within the management of the profession.

c. Ask questions that delve into what individuals like most and least about their jobs.

d. Track and share with your organization's volunteer leaders the trends directly and indirectly impacting members and the profession. Identify five to seven major areas that could have an effect in the next 12 to 24 months.

e. Look for opportunities to offer something that is distinctively different from what is currently being offered and solves a problem that exists within your space.

4. Help volunteer leaders make decisions based on data. Once an organization has collected feedback from different constituents, it's essential that it is shared with volunteer leaders, even highlighting the differences in how the organization's leadership may respond to various challenges. If strategic decisions are typically made by volunteer leaders and senior staff without data, an important voice may unintentionally be omitted from the discussion.

5. As you expand your reach or shift your attention to new audiences, change your value proposition accordingly. When OSCPA expanded its focus to include employers and non-CPAs, the value proposition needed to include offerings that would directly benefit the organization and not just the individual member. To identify opportunities to provide relevant value, engage new audiences in one-on-one interviews either over the phone or in person.

6. Don't be afraid to expand beyond or even move away from a value proposition that previously worked well, even if that value proposition is what the association was built upon. Not too long ago, associations were the primary providers of education, information, and networking. Today, members, prospects, and customers have many options to choose from that are free or inexpensive and more accessible. With

increased competition and the demand for more accessible and afford-able options, organizations need to find their unique spaces.

a. Who are the underserved populations within your industry? This may be your members' employers, supervisors, or even clients. Keep in mind, just because you are not serving an audience segment, doesn't mean their needs are not being met. If there is another association focused primarily on this market, this audience may provide opportunities to grow your customer base and non-dues revenue but not membership.

b. In which areas do you currently excel? Can you build upon name recognition and the strength of your brand? Does your organization have well-established relationships with key influencers and decision makers in the market?

c. What new distribution channels will you need to acquire or use to bring your offerings to the market? Many traditional retailers abandoned their efforts to compete with Amazon and instead used the platform to sell their products. While Amazon may not be the solution to expanding your distribution channels, you should consider its platform in your overall evaluation of how best to sell your products.

7. Once you've identified new opportunities to provide value, evaluate the skills, knowledge, and experience of your staff to identify gaps. You may need to add someone with industry knowledge and expertise to your team. If your organization promises a better, more customized experience, you may need to rethink every touchpoint from the web and mobile interactions through your front-line staff and beyond.

8. Examine the fault lines within your current portfolio. Be aware of the opportunity cost of providing programs and products that have become a commodity. Conduct an asset audit to examine your business model, member and nonmember needs, key performance metrics, awareness and position within the industry, and internal capabilities.

9. All members are not equal—don't treat them equally. In a traditional association model, every member typically has access to the same

benefits and are treated in the same way. In the for-profit world, many companies recognize the different levels of engagement or investment and reward those actions (think airline or hotel loyalty programs). Associations should consider a business model that better aligns and invests in program or product offerings where it has the greatest opportunity for impact and growth. This is not prioritizing profits over purpose; rather it is prioritizing relevance and influence over tradition.

Evaluating Product Lines

Maintaining a relevant and profitable business line is an essential component for any successful business plan. For primary product lines, such as your annual conference and tradeshow, publications, and certification programs, a list of questions similar to ones you need to answer for new product ideas should be answered annually.

1. What problem does the product solve?

2. What is unique about the product?

3. Why should members or customers look to the organization to fulfill the need?

4. Who is the target audience? Has it changed? Is it growing, shrinking, or staying the same?

5. What percentage of your members use or will use the product?

6. Will it be profitable, lose money, or break even after expenses?

7. Do the staff who work on the product have the skill set needed to keep it relevant and up to date?

8. Does the organization have the technology to deliver the product in a way that is accessible and affordable to current and future audiences?

9. Is the product mass marketed or do you customize your marketing to highlight the unique value proposition to each audience?

10. Do you routinely collect and analyze data on usage patterns to make improvements regularly?

•

CHAPTER 5

Become a Five-Star Organization Through Research

A five-star review for a product or service usually suggests the individual writing the testimonial was extremely satisfied with the overall experience (assuming he or she is not in some way paid by or otherwise associated with the product or service provider). The description of the product or service matched what he or she received, and it was delivered as expected. To earn a five-star review, your organization must develop a meaningful value proposition that begins with understanding the customer's journey as well as the problems he or she faces. And while this requires a strong commitment to frequently collecting and analyzing data, you must also request and respond to feedback so that you may continually improve. You may not make everyone happy, but if you are responsive and proactive, you'll know when and how to respond to market demands.

1. **Understand how your members and prospects have changed since your programs, products, and services were created.**

   a. What traits currently characterize your members?

   b. Are they mostly entrepreneurs? Are a growing number choosing to be employees rather than partners or owners?

   c. Are you seeing a major transition as baby boomers retire and the next generation of leaders move into senior management roles?

d. Do new leaders have the soft skills, training, and leadership qualities needed to succeed in their new roles?

e. Has the pathway to the profession changed from where it was 10, 15, or 20 years ago?

f. Are your members and prospects facing new competition?

g. Have your members' roles, influence, and responsibilities changed because of new regulations or advances in technology?

h. Have the skills and knowledge required to succeed in your profession changed? Have members' work environments, work hours, or other related factors changed?

2. **Identify emerging trends.**

a. What are the fads and emerging trends within your industry?

b. How will those trends affect your members, customers, and prospects?

c. What problems or challenges might these trends create within the profession?

d. What opportunities should members, prospects, and customers leverage to succeed in the next three to five years?

e. Will technology advancements change how individuals interact with your organization, programs, products, and services?

3. **Understand problems.**

a. In what situations are members and customers most likely to seek solutions?

b. What problems do they face today that didn't exist three years ago?

c. What information do they need to solve these problems?

d. Why do these problems exist?

e. What types of situations create these problems? Who is impacted by these challenges?

4. **Understand behaviors.**

    a. How and when is information and education consumed?

    b. How, when, and why do members and customers want to network?

    c. Do members or customers seek solutions at night after work? During a lunch break? While seeing a patient, customer, or client? Are they sitting at their desks, on their mobile phones, at the airport? Are they using high-speed internet?

    d. Do they want to connect with peers, colleagues, or others in-person or online? Should it be in a social setting?

5. **Look for gaps.** Identify the gaps in the marketplace—the white space that exists between what is currently offered and the unmet needs.

6. **Look for existing solutions.** Identify the problem solvers, individuals, and organizations that offer solutions.

    a. Who has the expertise, connections, influence, and solutions?

    b. Can it be repackaged?

    c. Can it be repurposed and distributed in a format that is more accessible, timely, and efficient?

7. **Create new concepts.** Failure *is* an option. Try, fail, learn, modify, create, track. Better yet, budget for innovation. When you budget for innovation rather than profits, you allow yourself to develop and test new ideas, fail, and refine the concept. If you budget for success, you are unlikely to take the risks needed to truly innovate.

When should your organization shift its strategies and tactics to ensure it is able to compete in today's market and respond to the changing needs of its members and customers? The answer lies in knowing everything you can about the profession, the industry, the pain points, and the opportunities—before your competitors and even your members. By conducting research on the state of the industry and monitoring internal trends as it relates to engagement, your organization will be in a better position to pivot when needed. And while not every initiative

Figure 1: Research Decision Tree

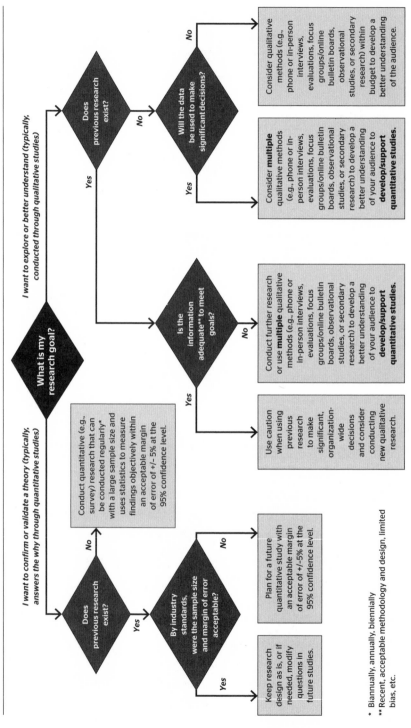

What is my research goal?

I want to confirm or validate a theory (typically, answers the why through quantitative studies)

I want to explore or better understand (typically, conducted through qualitative studies)

Does previous research exist? — No → Conduct quantitative (e.g., survey) research that can be conducted regularly* with a large sample size and uses statistics to measure findings objectively within an acceptable margin of error of +/- 5% at the 95% confidence level.

Does previous research exist? — Yes → **By industry standards, were the sample size and margin of error acceptable?**

- Yes → Keep research design as is, or if needed, modify questions in future studies.
- No → Plan for a future quantitative study with an acceptable margin of error of +/-5% at the 95% confidence level.

Does previous research exist? — Yes → **Is the information adequate** to meet goals?

- Yes → Use caution when using previous research to make significant, organization-wide decisions and consider conducting new qualitative research.
- No → Conduct further research or use **multiple** qualitative methods (e.g., phone or in-person interviews, focus groups/online bulletin boards, observational studies, or secondary research) to develop a better understanding of your audience to **develop/support quantitative studies.**

Does previous research exist? — No → **Will the data be used to make significant decisions?**

- Yes → Consider **multiple** qualitative methods (e.g., phone or in-person interviews, focus groups/online bulletin boards, observational studies, or secondary research) to develop a better understanding of your audience to **develop/support quantitative studies.**
- No → Consider qualitative methods (e.g., phone or in-person interviews, focus groups/online bulletin boards, observational studies, or secondary research) within budget to develop a better understanding of the audience.

* Biannually, annually, biennially

** Recent, acceptable methodology and design, limited bias, etc.

requires a major research study, it is helpful to understand when and what types of research should be collected if you wish to become a five-star organization.

The question of how you build an effective business model and a five-star organization should be addressed by answering how you will differentiate yourself, according to Jean-Paul Guilbault, president and CEO of Community Brands, a company that provides technology and engagement platforms to membership organizations, schools, and nonprofits to help them better manage mission-critical operations and relationships. Guilbault explained, "On one level, the question of a business model is a dissection of lots of little questions. How are you going to make money? How are you going to deliver value? Who is the target audience? What is the sweet spot within the target audience? What is the internal cost structure? But what's fundamentally changing the conversation is the consumer response to what you offer and how you price it."

One of the challenges associations face, according to Guilbault, is an aversion to change even though the behaviors and attitudes of their audience are becoming episodic and experience-seeking in terms of what and when they will engage. To engage members, Guilbault suggested organizations increase their investment in digital technology to increase micro opportunities to connect. "Our research showed that organizations that have invested in the technology to meet the needs of today's members are seeing exponentially higher renewal and satisfaction rates. It must be 'mobile first' in everything you do."

Another area that needs attention and will provide a return on the investment is making sure your organization has a good understanding of technology and the use of the data signals being sent by members and customers. If you have a bias for using data, a culture that embraces experimentation, and limited technology customizations, you will be more likely to see the payoff in your technology investment. Guilbault stated, "Every CEO should really take a hard look at their technology and ask a lot of questions about customization. Customization will be the biggest handcuff for organizations to respond to change or evolve. Technology will never be 100 percent, but customizing is almost certain to cost more in the long run, be it hard costs or lack of speed to adjust." Guilbault firmly believes the path to relevance, engagement, and retention is through gaining a greater understanding of the needs and expectations of your audience and creating an emotional experience that will reinforce the value. "We have to create value with the experience and memory, not just the product," said Guilbault.

Figure 2: Examples of Industry Research Conducted by Associations

Type of Research	Association	Example
State of the Industry	National Restaurant Association	• State of the Industry • State of Restaurant Sustainability • Facts at a Glance • State Statistics
	Society of Gynecologic Oncology	• State of the Profession
	Health Information and Management Systems Society (HIMSS)	• Outpatient Practice Management and Electronic Health Records Study
Trends and Forecast	National Restaurant Association	• What's Hot Culinary Forecast • Restaurant TrendMapper • Global Palates • Restaurant Industry 2020 • Consumer Spending in Restaurants
	HIMSS	• Healthcare IT Demand Forecasts Study
	Medical Group Management Association (MGMA)	• Telehealth: Adoption and Best Practices • The Rising Trend of Nonphysician Provider Utilization in Healthcare
Economic Forecast	National Restaurant Association	• Restaurant Economic Forecast • Economist's Notebook
Technology	National Restaurant Association	• Mapping the Technology Landscape
	HIMSS	• Mobile Study on Usage in U.S. Hospitals • Inpatient Telemedicine Study

Type of Research	Association	Example
Performance and Operations	National Restaurant Association	• Restaurant Operations Report • Restaurant Performance Index
	HIMSS	• Leadership Study
Quick Polls	MGMA	• MGMA weekly polls on human resources, financial management, operations, and health information technology
Benchmarking Reports	MGMA	• Compensation Data • Practice Operations Data
	HIMSS	• Compensation Survey

Making the Case for Advocacy Support (Hint: It's All About Value)

As president and CEO of the American Beverage Association (ABA), Susan Neely, CAE, oversees an organization that is a vital part of the U.S. economy. With America's nonalcoholic beverage industry providing nearly 253,000 jobs and creating an economic impact of $182.6 billion, ABA strives to unite this iconic industry. And while the organization serves the industry by providing a unified voice, it has taken a much larger role in helping provide the data needed to inform decisions that affect its members' brands and bottom lines.

When Neely arrived at ABA, its annual budget hovered around $10 million. Today, Neely has grown the financial resources of the organization closer to $80 million by shifting its business strategy to focus on efforts that improved the value proposition—and garnered the necessary financial support from members to drive those efforts forward. Neely explained, "When I came on board, there was a sense by the board that the environment they were doing business in was changing dramatically. The major members of this organization own trademarks that are more than 100 years old and are some of the most recognized and valued brands in the world. In the past, all they needed to do was to make a safe, good tasting beverage and engage in community service and community support. Those days were changing. Public policy was impacting this. The members understood there needed to be a change within the trade association that was representing their interests."

As a first step, Neely used public opinion research with consumer groups, members of the public health community, and others to address policy challenges. Although the initial goal was to establish pathways to the position the nonalcoholic beverage industry held in the past—that of well-respected brands that were loved by consumers—it was also important to help members learn how best to address consumers' current concerns. "Our members believe in listening to consumers and consumer segments. Doing market research is fundamental to how they conduct business. For the ABA, it helped us demonstrate that we were being strategic and would work with them to achieve our goals," Neely said. Conducting this type of research so that her members could be more responsive to the concerns and changing consumer attitudes was an essential part of the organization's success.

To understand the shift in how ABA approached its role and helped shape a new message platform and unified voice of the nonalcoholic beverage industry, let's travel back to the beginning of Neely's tenure with the organization. The story begins with the threat of a class action lawsuit brought by the Center for Science in the Public Interest against The Coca-Cola Company, PepsiCo, Cadbury Schweppes, and their bottlers, and it ends with an agreement facilitated by President Clinton, Arkansas Governor Huckabee (R), and the American Heart Association. According to a 2005 report published by the Government Accountability Office, almost half of all public schools had exclusive contracts with beverage companies, and the contracts were promoted as providing a source of revenue for schools.[1] However, a public health advocacy group in Oregon countered that very little money went to the schools.[2]

To address this issue and to provide a solution that would be accepted by the members of the trade association and the organization filing the lawsuit, Neely invested time and money in consumer research. "We started testing different ideas and one idea was, 'Should we change the way we're selling our beverages in school?' From our focus groups and consumer research, we learned that parents who have children in the K-12 space were supportive of having our beverages sold in schools, but they wanted guardrails based on the age of their children. When they couldn't be present and guide the choices of younger children, they wanted limited offerings—milk, water, 100 percent juice. For high school students, they wanted their teenage children to have choices, but they wanted them to be lower calorie choices."

From that research, ABA developed a voluntary policy to guide its members in decisions regarding what beverages were sold in schools. Neely recalled, "After working with President Clinton and the Heart Association, we agreed to change the mix of our beverages nationally within three school years. With the nutritional scientists at the AHA, we developed a set of standards of what the mix should look like. Our members had to retrofit machines to fit the new package sizes. They also had to reformulate products—and in some cases, innovate new ones." On May 6, 2006, ABA announced a memorandum of understanding that ABA along with the three leading beverage competitors were signing with the Alliance for a Healthier Generation. On the morning of their announcement, some of the organizations that had been considering filing the class action lawsuit said they would not proceed. "That was an early success. It created a model for how we work as ABA, and we continue to look for leadership platforms with future administrations," Neely said. After the three-year implementation period, members had reduced beverage calories shipped to schools by 88 percent—a number that has since increased to more than 90 percent.

Under Neely's leadership, ABA pivoted its approach to how it addressed the challenges faced by its members and the industry. "We set up an ombudsman to make sure all competitors were upholding the agreed-upon standards. We understood that it was important to provide our members with the needed support to implement as individual companies and be successful as a collective industry," she explained. This led to a new advertising campaign where ABA told the story of the initiative. It was the first time Coke and Pepsi agreed to have their products in the same advertisement together. Neely cannot imagine this happening in years prior. By having the competitors appear together, it became believable, and it led to other opportunities. With the success of this initiative, Neely and her team were able to demonstrate the value of membership and the importance of making a financial commitment to the organization. For example, the website BalanceUS.org tells the industry's story of how it supports consumers' efforts to balance what they eat, drink, and do. It showcases the industry's efforts to help cut sugar in the American diet by reducing beverage calories per person nationally. The site also explains how the beverage industry is creating jobs, working with local partners, and giving back to support healthier communities.

Through research, public awareness, and community building, the American Beverage Association focused its business model on addressing the challenges its members faced, and members then increased their commitments to and investments in the organization. As their investments grew and as the organization continued to provide a valuable service to the industry, ABA's revenue grew.

ABA was able to demonstrate that through greater member support, it could accomplish more for the industry at-large, as well as its customers and consumers, than any one company could achieve on its own. From working to reduce sugar in the American diet to driving sustainable solutions to preserve the environment, Neely and her team understood that they were uniquely positioned to help the industry thrive during a time of rapid change.

(As of May 2018, Neely announced she would be joining ACLI as president and CEO.)

Lessons Learned From ABA

1. Become an essential partner to your members' success by investing in a value proposition that will garner stronger support. The investment may not immediately deliver a financial reward to the organization, and as such, you must allow time for the investment to demonstrate value. By conducting research on behalf of the industry, sharing the findings, and communicating how the industry was addressing public concerns, the American Beverage Association reinforced its role as an essential partner. The association was uniquely positioned to provide the guidance needed to help its members address the quickly changing behaviors and concerns of consumers.

2. Dedicate resources to learning more. Research and data should serve as a cornerstone to your organization's business strategy—especially when you are ready to pivot your focus to remain relevant. From identifying

gaps or unfilled needs to staying on top of consumer and business trends, research can lessen the risk an organization takes by providing insight into what is needed and why issues raised are of a concern to your audience and their customers or clients.

3. Don't shy away from addressing issues head-on. Take a leadership role and be the unifying voice for the industry. By taking on the major challenges that one member alone cannot afford to tackle, you will demonstrate why it is worthwhile for members to invest in the organization. For example, instead of redirecting the conversation regarding the amount of sugar in Americans' diets, the American Beverage Association built a coalition of three of the biggest competitors— Coca-Cola, Pepsi, and Dr Pepper—to help families find balance. From industry reports to creating the National School Beverage Guidelines, under Neely's leadership, ABA helped reduce beverage calories shipped to schools by 90 percent between 2004 and the 2009–2010 school year.[3] ABA's role in bringing together fierce competitors helped reinforce its value in the eyes of its members.

The Last Mile

The game changer for most organizations will be improving how content is delivered and providing solutions that fit the situation in which they will be used. And while it is important to provide trustworthy and unbiased information, organizations that can deliver information that has been optimized to get the job done will become essential to their members and customers. Unfortunately, some of the characteristics that strengthen an organization's brand reputation also create some challenges. In a recent study conducted by Avenue M Group for a medical organization, we found that when selecting a resource to stay informed or find an answer to a question, physicians view those developed by the professional society as being trustworthy and scientifically rigorous/graded but not necessarily easy to use. In fact, the study revealed physicians are more likely to use UpToDate, a software system that is a point-of-care medical resource, in some situations because it offers a broader range of topics, offers better search functionality, and is easier to use.

Where should organizations begin to address such a challenge? The first step in understanding members' and customers' needs is to dive deeper into specific situations or challenges they face in their daily work and to identify the resources they use to help solve problems. For example, you can ask members and customers to identify the resource they are most likely to use in a variety of situations (see Table 1). For healthcare professionals, it may be at the point of care. For a restaurant owner, it may be a solution that is easy to use in the kitchen or when managing the front of the house.

Next, organizations need to determine how responses differ by audience segment. This may include demographics such as experience, work setting, location, or other factors. It should also include a review of the issues being faced by underserved markets. Disruptive innovations in the consumer world frequently arise from providing products and services to individuals who have been ignored or disregarded because they are not as profitable or are not central to the core audience.[4]

Table 1: Which resource are you most likely to use in each situation?

	Association	Competitor	No resource
I need an answer to a specific question to make a decision.			
I need to review all facets of a specific topic to inform decisions.			
I don't have a lot of knowledge or experience with a topic and need to learn more about it.			
I want to access only evidence-based guidelines to inform decisions.			
I need to access "how tos" to gain more experience on a specific topic.			
I need to find a quick answer to a question to resolve an immediate concern.			

Keep in mind, members and customers can only express their opinions on how they currently access information and resources. What's missing from this type of research is how likely they are to use a product or service that doesn't yet exist. To create new products and services or deliver a better business model around your current portfolio, you need to examine the reasons why problems exist. It's the *why* behind the *what.*

Consider the following scenario: It's been two years since you launched a new educational program, and your attendance or revenue has fallen far short of projections. The organization's leadership is considering pulling the plug on the initiative. Prior to the launch, you conducted a survey to identify interest in the topic, barriers to attendance, pricing thresholds, and the best time and location to host the program. Anecdotally, you've heard your volunteer leaders express how important it is for the organization to be a thought leader on this topic and the leading source of information. You've used multiple channels to promote your program and feel confident the issue isn't a lack of awareness. So, what went wrong? If this scenario sounds familiar, you are not alone. In fact, nearly every organization I've worked with has shared a similar story about a program, product, or service that failed to launch, break even, or turn a profit even if the data supported its existence.

To figure out what went wrong, let's begin with time to market. If your organization requires new programs or products go through an extensive vetting process that hinges on quarterly committee meetings, extensive research, and approval from the volunteer leaders before they can be launched, it's likely that your new idea was no longer new when it hit the market. The same is true for updating products as well as creating new delivery channels to bring products to market. And while you may argue that some ideas require a high level of rigor before your brand can be associated with the product, slowness to market may also blemish your brand reputation.

A second constraint that could cause a failure to launch is zero or low tolerance for failure. Most organizations operate on a lean budget, one that must be submitted, reviewed, and approved well in advance of the start of the fiscal year. Projections for revenue and engagement are submitted and programs are evaluated based on the likelihood they will achieve the necessary targets. However, what if your organization budgeted for failure? What if you set aside 3 to 5 percent of your budget to beta test new ideas with the goal of fail fast, learn, improve, and rebuild?

Most successful entrepreneurs will tell you they had more ideas fail than succeed. A quote commonly attributed to Thomas Edison is "I have not failed. I just found 10,000 ways that won't work." Associations do not need to test 10,000 ideas, but they should at least be allowed to succeed at the same rate as a professional baseball player who bats .300. In other words, if you develop and launch 10 ideas and three succeed, you are far better off than if you are too slow, too late, or not even in the game.

It's the last mile of the journey that many organizations pay too little attention to when developing programs, products, and services for their members and customers. If your benefits do not help members progress or solve a problem, then they will be passed over for another resource that does. Create and provide the tools and information needed—and deliver it in a way that is most accessible. Just creating and offering tools and information, even ones that are highly rated and well respected, are not enough in today's market. To build a sustainable business model based on relevancy, connectedness, diversity, and inclusion, your organization must remove barriers to using your programs, products, and services and continually invest in new ideas that can be easily accessed at the point of use.

Using Research to Select a Membership Model

Though you shouldn't wait until you have 100 percent of the research before acting on an idea, it is crucial to make data-driven decisions. As Robert E. Gunther writes as truth number 29 in his book *The Truth About Making Smart Decisions*, "Get 80 percent (or less) of what you need, and then act on it."[5] Examining the behaviors and motivations of members and customers through research and data mining is the key to developing programs, products, and services that provide value. Research is also the foundation for building a membership model that reflects and supports the mission of the association.

Ultimately, if your organization wishes to synchronize value and cost while maintaining or encouraging growth, it must consider a membership model that leverages its strengths, eliminates barriers, and addresses the needs of the changing environment. You must also build a model that is nimble and customizable based on immediate needs and interests. To achieve these goals, conduct research to answer the following questions, some of which were introduced in Chapter 4:

- What are the low, medium, and high drivers of membership and engagement?

- Are members aware of your benefits? How satisfied are they when engaging with the organization, either by accessing information or expanding their knowledge and education? How does satisfaction with key benefits affect renewal rates?

- What are the next best alternatives in the marketplace, and how do they compare to your offerings? Are the next best alternatives more affordable or accessible?

- What are the top challenges and issues facing members, and how does that impact the decision to engage with your organization and other organizations? What issues do they expect to influence their work in the next three years?

- Why do some members join and become actively involved while others engage at much lower levels or allow their memberships to lapse? How does this differ by audience segment and behavior?

- What are the unserved segments within your community? Do they have different needs than your core audience? Would they be interested in your current programs, products, and services if they were made accessible? Is this audience large enough to support a business model that offered a lower price benefits package based on access and usage of specific benefits?

- How do members currently consume information? What trends are emerging in the consumer world that could affect how members and customers wish to interact with your organization? How does this differ by audience segment?

- What programs, products, and services could be enhanced, changed, or improved to increase the value of membership? Are there gaps in the current solutions offered that could be filled through creating new benefits?

- Who do you engage in the decision-making process when the organization is considering developing new products or updating existing ones? Do your committees, councils, and task forces reflect the diversity of your audience? If you include early career professionals or individuals from outside your country or region, do they have an equal voice in the decision-making process?

Selecting the Best Membership Model

Creating a new membership model is not the same as creating a new business model. Rather, a membership model is part of the overall design that helps organizations successfully achieve their mission. A fully developed business model identifies and solves a customer's challenge by delivering value. For some organizations, 100 percent of their customers are members. However, most organizations provide value to customers, members, partners, the public, and others. For nonprofits to achieve their missions, the business model should be designed in a way that enables the organization to maximize revenue and reach, and a membership model that is aligned with value is a crucial component.

Every model carries a level of risk, including the membership model your organization has in place today (assuming you have members). Although your current model may have served the organization well, if today's members and prospects do not find enough value, many will allow their memberships to lapse or remain customers rather than join. The model your organization selects or maintains should be based on the primary goals of the organization and the goals of membership. For example, your organization may be looking to achieve one or all of the following goals: financial sustainability; membership growth; increased usage of programs, products, and services; or expansion into new markets or deeper within existing markets. The challenge is prioritizing the goals as this will guide the decision making when considering a new membership structure for your organization.

Barriers are another area to consider. Based on trends my company has observed in membership surveys, two major barriers that prevent individuals from joining an organization are cost and the perception that there isn't enough value. Additionally, individuals and companies may already be invested in another organization that provides overlapping value. When they consider the return on the investment, they may determine it makes more sense to remain a customer.

Most organizations have some transactional members. In my experience this number is typically between 20 and 30 percent of the current member base. Transactional members will evaluate the difference between the member and nonmember rates for the products and services they use. If they are not using a member discount, such as attending your annual conference at the member rate, and if they are not actively engaged with the organization, they may allow their memberships to lapse. Other members may join while they are in the process of studying for an exam or certification. Once they've passed the exam, the value of membership may drop if their primary interest was only in receiving a heavily discounted rate on exam preparation materials. Transactional members will always exist. Not every member needs to be fully engaged. In fact, your organization most likely has members who feel connected even if they are not engaged. They read your journals or newsletters or use some of your resources, but if they were to receive an engagement score, it might be lower than one would expect of a member who is satisfied and connected. Associations need to adjust their business strategies to ensure transactional and connected members are valued. With these caveats in mind, which is the right model for your organization?

Tiered Membership Design

A tiered membership structure is designed to increase the number of options that will appeal to prospective and current members and provide a reasonable alternative to the concept of one-size-fits-all. In a multilevel membership structure, the lowest tier should eliminate a barrier for new members but not jeopardize the financial stability of the organization. To offer an entry-level tier of membership, your organization must determine the potential size of the market and how many members are needed at this level to break even in terms of cost and revenue. To make tiered membership less financially risky (e.g., if a high percentage of members who had been paying the regular dues rate downgrade their membership), organizations should complete two steps.

First, determine the percentage of current members who use various benefits. For example, if your organization has the data to prove that 30 percent of its members consistently register for a program or conference and take advantage of the member discount, you may be able to project, at a minimum, that they are likely to remain in a membership category that includes member discounts on programs—if the difference in price is equal to or provides even greater savings.

Second, consider what bundles of benefits will move prospective members to join at each level. If your organization allows nonmembers to access most of your information and resources via your website, it may be difficult to recruit them to join your organization unless some of the relevant information they are seeking is behind a paywall and they cannot obtain the information or tools from another source.

Additionally, creating a tiered membership structure may help your organization provide an enhanced level of access and benefits to individuals who wish to support the association and industry beyond the regular membership level. At this premium level, you may need to identify new experiences or offer a higher level of service to recruit and retain members.

A tiered membership model provides more flexibility and choice for current and prospective members. If you mine your existing data, you can recommend the best tier of membership based on the level of involvement by similar members. For example, you may see a trend that members in the beginning of their careers are more likely to attend courses to help them prepare for a certification or gain the skills they need to advance to a management position. By examining the usage patterns of current members by demographics such as career stage, employer type, or other factors, you could actively promote specific benefits based on the tier of membership. This could help increase the relevancy of membership and the likelihood of renewal.

Two-Tier Membership Models

There are two approaches an organization can take when considering a two-tier membership model. The first is a low-high tiered program. With this model, the organization offers limited benefits at the lower level. For example, an organization may call the lower level a subscription and only provide access to digital resources through its website. All other benefits—for example, the ability to volunteer, speak, receive member discounts, and serve on committees, councils, or the board—require full membership. The second option is a medium-high tiered program. The medium tier of membership would be similar to a flat-dues structure in terms of price and benefits. The higher tier, however, would be offered to members interested in becoming more involved or receiving benefits or experiences limited to a select number of members. For example, benefits may include recognition, receptions, or pre-release access to important publications. It's important for an organization to identify and test a variety of unique benefits members may value enough to join the higher membership category.

A two-tier program is often the simplest approach, easiest to manage internally, and easiest to communicate to members and prospects. If successful, it can provide the organization with additional dues revenue. While it is the least risky option, it may not provide enough incentive for prospects and customers to join.

Three-Tier Membership Models

A three-tier membership model combines elements of the two two-tier options of low-high and medium-high into three membership levels: basic (or starter), full, and premium. It provides individuals and organizations that have financial constraints with a viable option (i.e., the basic or starter level) while meeting the needs of those members who desire a first-class experience (i.e., the premium level). The basic or first tier is the most budget friendly. In terms of pricing and benefits, some organizations scale it back to bare minimums in hopes of capturing a larger share of the market. An alternative to basic is a starter category, a low-priced option that includes full benefits for the first few years of membership. To limit the financial risk of members dropping to the lowest category, your organization could restrict the starter membership to new graduates or individuals who are new to the association (even if they have been in the field for a number of years). Such a category provides prospects with an opportunity to sample the value proposition before committing to a full membership.

A disadvantage of having a starter membership level instead of a basic membership is that it doesn't offer a low-cost option for individuals who aren't new to the association but are having difficulty justifying the cost of membership. Such members may still support the organization's mission and wish to maintain some level of affiliation, but if the value they are receiving doesn't match the cost, they may allow their memberships to lapse and return only as customers. This disadvantage may grow if more employers stop paying for or reimbursing employees' association membership dues.

If you choose a three-tier structure, do not assume most current members will gravitate to full membership, the middle level, just because it is the most similar to the flat-dues structure. Be prepared for an exodus to the lower tier. Before implementing this model, conduct financial modeling to determine how many members you will need to attract to break even and what benefits should be offered at each tier.

With a small price differential between the tiers, your organization can minimize the risks of implementing this model. This type of pricing model is most frequently used in the consumer marketplace. If you've recently bought popcorn at a movie theater, you may recall seeing three options based on size and price. The price differential is often set so that if you pay just a little bit more, you will receive a much larger tub of popcorn. Most consumers are likely to pick the middle bucket of popcorn because they feel they get the most value for their money and will not waste money on something they won't finish.

Group Membership Programs

Many organizations are moving to a new membership model that allows organizations to pay membership dues for all employees under a group billing program, often offered at a discount. The simplified billing program is attractive to employers, especially if the association can provide information on how much the employer saved during the past 12 months due to discounts on education and product purchases.

In recent years, I've seen a number of organizations expand their benefit offerings and create new services based on the needs of the employer and not solely the individual member. For example, many employers have cited talent recruitment and management as one of the biggest challenges they face. As part of the membership package, associations are now either developing new programs or partnering with existing companies to custom deliver talent recruitment and management programs on-site or online to organizations that join their group membership programs.

CHAPTER 6

•

The Sharing Economy

It usually begins with a simple request: "May I use your user name and password? I need to order something." A friend or family member may ask to borrow your login credentials to order something from a website. Or a co-worker may ask to use your login information to access a resource or purchase a product from an association where you maintain membership. Sometimes it occurs because employers will only pay for membership in one association, even if numerous organizations serve the profession. Or an employer may pay for an association membership for one person but not an entire department. It happens because there simply isn't enough value for your co-worker to pay the full price of membership out of his or her own pocket, but occasionally he or she needs to buy a product. If this doesn't happen among your peers, you can be fairly confident that it happens among young professionals within your organization.

While not all benefits are shareable, access to content and information via a members-only section on a website is easy to share. Physicians may allow their colleagues or other members of their healthcare team to use their member IDs when placing an order for practice resources or a coding manual. Anecdotally, I've heard stories of parents sharing their Netflix account with adult children who have recently moved out and are living on a tight budget and of Amazon Prime members ordering items for family members to share the perk of free two-day shipping. Like I said, people share their memberships.

There are some advantages to allowing or even encouraging individuals to share their memberships, including the potential for increased sales. With Amazon Household, for example, two adult and up to four teen and four child profiles may link in a household. Two adults in a household can share digital content, and teen logins allow teenagers to shop on their own with parental approval via text. Family members can share e-books, audiobooks, apps, games, photo albums, streaming access to Prime Video, and free two-day delivery benefits. Amazon gently nudges its Prime members to officially share their memberships by promoting its Amazon Household option at the bottom of order confirmations.

Imagine what would happen if your organization used the same tactic and actively encouraged members to share their memberships with colleagues and friends. Even if some restrictions applied, it could increase your reach, increase sales, and increase the overall value of membership. By creating an option to legitimately share membership with colleagues, organizations could identify prospects and their buying behavior and better serve the needs of this market. It may be unrealistic to believe that everyone within a company or organization will see the value in paying for membership. Based on their position or interest area, they may not believe it holds enough relevancy to their daily role and responsibilities. However, a shared option may provide enough value for them to become a repeat customer.

Of course, this isn't an easy solution to implement. It requires a thorough assessment of the size of your audience and current market share. You will need to have a deep understanding of your primary, secondary, and tertiary markets and their needs and examine the financial model to price it appropriately. But if your organization is pivoting to focus on reach or revenue, this may be an option to explore. If the priority is reach rather than revenue, a sharing option may be worth considering for loss-leader programs that are not revenue generators but create valuable connections with individuals who have a strong interest in a specific topic, product, or focus area.

Badge Sharing

A few years ago, I flew from Chicago to Salt Lake City to attend a conference. One of the first things that greeted me when I walked up to the registration counter was a sign announcing it was against the rules to share a conference badge. Aside from the fact that it wasn't the most welcoming way to greet an attendee after a long flight, the sign highlighted a policy that feels out of touch with the business models many companies are using today. While some organizations offer both multiday and single-day registration passes, most do not allow attendees to share their badges with a colleague or friend.

In the association community, there are a few reasons why an organization may restrict attendees from sharing a badge. Many organizations believe they will lose money if attendees share a badge. Some organizations maintain a strict policy prohibiting the sharing of a registration because they provide continuing education credits to attendees. I've also observed restrictions on who may attend a conference based on an employer type or position (e.g., physicians only or nonvendors). However, like most policies that have been in place for years or even decades, it's time for organizations to review badge policies that place unnecessary limitations on their ability to expand their reach.

Whether it is providing registrants with continuing education credits or requiring attendees to be employed in certain positions, associations often list the obstacles to making changes to their policies. Instead of focusing on the reasons why you can't change a policy, focus on how you could adjust the policy to meet changing behaviors or changes in the industry. Using continuing education as an example, could your organization put safeguards in place to ensure only individuals who attend every session or every day of the conference receive the continuing education credit? Rigidly adhering to a business model that restricts engagement is not the solution. Instead, expand the options for allowing attendees to share their registrations, but restrict some of the tangible benefits such as a certification or continuing education credits. The advantages of increasing attendance by offering a more flexible model is one that should be examined and considered, especially by associations concerned about stagnant or declining meeting attendance.

The desire to share a meeting registration with a colleague typically occurs among individuals who live within driving distance of the event. It is unlikely that someone will pay for airfare and hotel, which together will exceed the costs of the conference, but will not be willing to pay the registration fee. I've observed that many employers will reimburse educational expenses, while fewer pay for related travel expenses. In looking at your meeting data, how many participants are within driving distance? Based on the data, what is the real likelihood of a negative financial impact in offering a legitimate sharing option? How does that compare to the value of increased reach if a company within driving distance of your meeting could afford to send more employees through a badge-sharing program?

The following is a practical example of how to boost attendance and increase your reach using a sharing economy business model. When a healthcare organization asked me to help it attract c-level executives to its conference, our research indicated the primary barriers were time and relevancy. Many of the executives we interviewed did not have the time to attend a multiday conference, even one that was being hosted less than 20 minutes from their institutions. A quick look at the organization's meeting agenda also revealed only a few sessions could possibly attract this audience segment. It was clear that the driving factor in the decision not to attend the conference wasn't the conference fee but the return on investment. It is hard to justify paying a full conference fee when you may be able to attend only a few sessions. Combine that with the demands on their time, it was unlikely the organization could attract c-level executives to its conference unless it created a value proposition aligned with the needs and behavior of this audience. In other words, it needed to create a value proposition and business model designed with the customer in mind, not the organization.

After reviewing the agenda, the organization added a few sessions that were customized for c-level healthcare executives and would be delivered by a peer. We also recommended creating a shared registration fee. The member rate for the three-day conference was $995. The nonmember rate was $1,495, and the shared badge rate for three days for members was $1,195. The only requirement with the shared badge was that one attendee had to be a member of the organization. The new categories were available to anyone but were heavily promoted to individuals within a 50-mile radius of the meeting. The messages focused on relevancy, value, and flexibility. By allowing members to share their badges, the organization was able to attract more individuals to its conference. Although their focus had been on c-level executives, the same approach would work well for other audience segments, including early career professionals.

A Castle, a Treehouse, or a One-Bedroom Apartment in the City?

Planning a trip to Boston? You have an endless array of choices for accommodations. From luxury condos near the Boston Harbor to one-bedroom apartments in the Back Bay, there is an option for any price point and experience. Airbnb was one of the first companies to capitalize on the sharing economy in 2008, and by 2018, it has nearly 5 million listings in 81,000 cities and 191 countries[1]—more listings than the five largest hotel chains combined.[2] Within 10 years, more than 300 million guest arrivals had been logged through the Airbnb website or mobile app. By going through Airbnb, you can stay in one of 3,000 castles or one of 1,400 treehouses. Yet the company owns no inventory. Instead, Airbnb built a technology platform that enables millions of people around the world to monetize their homes and "become hospitality entrepreneurs."[3] You don't need to contact Airbnb to reserve a room, check on available inventory, or change a reservation. The mobile experience provides all of the information you need whether you are a first-time user or a repeat visitor. As a company, Airbnb makes money from its service fees.

Like many of the companies profiled in this book, Airbnb's value proposition is built around a digital and physical component. To ensure the company evolves and to meet the needs of its diverse audience, Airbnb's business model is based on four beliefs: autonomy, data, experimentation, and diversity. The company views data as "the voice of our consumer at scale."[4] Describing itself as a "test and learn" culture, Airbnb encourages experimentation, and the company says its mission-driven teams consist of a diversity of skills, knowledge, experiences, and backgrounds. Any organization, regardless of its stage of maturity, can be nimble if it values the input from a diverse culture. Embracing diversity of backgrounds and experiences at the decision-making level within an organization is one example of this idea in action. Ensuring different perspectives are not only heard, but valued, and when taken into consideration, will increase the likelihood of obtaining meaningful and relevant input on an ongoing basis.

Airbnb's platform uses predictive analytics and machine learning to instantly evaluate signals and investigate suspicious activity. Hosts in the United States must pass a background check, and a secure platform is used to ensure payments are safely made. And if you encounter a problem, a global team is available 24/7 to help. It's the model of how the sharing economy provides consumers with more options when traveling. If you are a property owner, Airbnb gives you an opportunity to earn revenue when your home is not being used.

People have been sharing their assets for centuries. Airbnb did not create the concept of connecting travelers and hosts. Rather, it created a platform to better manage the transaction of peer-to-peer exchanges— and it did so at a time when the market was ripe for an alternative to the current offerings of hotel chains and rental properties. As unique and disruptive as the business model may appear, the concept isn't new. Airbnb owes much of its success to leveraging several key technology advancements at a time when consumers and property owners were looking for alternative options.

When Airbnb first opened its doors as AirBed&Breakfast in 2008, the economy was in a tailspin. By the end of 2008, the National Bureau of Economic Research announced the United States was in a recession, beginning from December 2007.[5] On March 5, 2009, the Dow Jones industrial average dropped 53.4 percent.[6] Adding to the financial uncertainty of the time, the national unemployment rate jumped from 5 percent in December 2007 to 9.5 percent in June 2009, peaking at 10 percent by October 2009.[7] The market was clearly ready for a new way to save money when traveling and to earn money as a homeowner.

Although Airbnb built a successful business model, it's not the first couch-surfing platform. And it proved that you don't need to be the first to be the most successful. By 2020, Airbnb believes it will gross $3.5 billion, which is more than 85 percent of the Fortune 500 companies.[8] Some lessons we can learn from its business model:

1. Ease of use is essential. It's easy to book a room or an experience. The entire process from finding and reviewing a rental property to communicating with homeowners and submitting payment has been simplified through the use of a well-designed platform accessible on any device.

2. Referrals are a powerful marketing tool. Airbnb has grown organically through reviews and referrals. Before reserving and paying for a rental, you can scroll through a variety of highly personal reviews that offer specific details on what was most loved (or in some cases disliked) about the rental. Even when you consider purchasing a new item on Amazon, you're unlikely to buy it unless it's received a high number of positive reviews.

3. Ensure data drives decisions. The company relies heavily on data to make decisions regarding enhancements and areas for expansion. Once its initial concept succeeded within specific geographic locations and audience segments, the company expanded into areas that mirrored these data points. It continues to collect feedback from hosts and users to make improvements and enhance the service.

4. Your mission reflects your value. Airbnb's mission speaks to why people make the decision to use the service to find a place to stay: "belong anywhere."[9] It focuses on community and relationships and provides a tangible benefit that is directly connected to its mission. Airbnb's branding does not stray from its mission and purpose—and subsequently, it quickly created a following. What makes Airbnb different from other sharing economy businesses is its focus on humanity rather than on transactional situations. The experience you have when you stay in another person's home, unlike what you may feel when you get a ride to the airport from Lyft, is a "shared" experience. Airbnb is about creating unique shared experiences that cannot be found anywhere else. It's what differentiates it from a stay at a hotel.

5. Don't fear failure. Failure is built into the DNA of Airbnb. Despite having been told the idea would never succeed, the founders

invested their time, energy, and passion into creating a business they believed would fill a void and provide an affordable alternative to traditional offerings in the marketplace.

6. Timing is everything. Prior to Airbnb, other companies offered a platform for individuals to find and rent vacation homes. When Airbnb first launched, the economy had just entered the Great Recession. People were looking for opportunities to make money from their unused space while others were looking to save money and reduce their travel expenses.

Are Your Benefits Parked 95 Percent of the Time?

Once Airbnb became a household name, it didn't take long for the concept of the sharing economy—or more accurately the access economy—to spread to other areas, including car sharing. Building upon the idea shared by many urban planners and transportation advisors that most cars are parked 95 percent of the time,[10] the appeal of peer-to-peer car sharing focuses on a number of trends within the auto industry. As the largest generation since baby boomers, millennials are the obvious target for automobile manufacturers and sellers. However, the trend is toward this group buying cars out of necessity rather than as a rite of passage or status symbol. When you combine the high level of student debt and changing attitudes toward car ownership, it's not surprising that car-sharing programs are popping up in many major cities across the United States. "Millennials buy cars more pragmatically ... They are forever going to be more on the pragmatic car-as-commodity, car-as-appliance part of the equation," said John Paul MacDuffie, a professor of management at The Wharton School, University of Pennsylvania.[11] Having grown up in an environment where they have the option to pay for the services they need, when they need them, using a car-sharing service will serve millennials well until their needs change. Car owners, therefore, can maximize the return on their investment by earning revenue when their cars would otherwise be parked in their garages.

The concept of "parked" benefits is applicable to many associations. One example is the annual meeting. For organizations who provide most of their membership value through member discounts to an annual meeting, the annual meeting may be a "parked" benefit for those unable to attend every year, and some members choose to drop their membership for the years when they cannot attend. By offering flexible access options to the annual meeting (e.g., recordings of sessions available online, opportunities to engage remotely), associations enable members who are unable to attend the meeting in person to take advantage of a benefit that would otherwise be "parked." Another example is private online communities. For some associations' online communities, the majority of rank-and-file members may use that benefit infrequently or only when they have a question. To increase the value of the online community, an association can enlist volunteers to regularly curate helpful answers or advice and re-package them into accessible content in the newsletter. Most associations have core benefits that their average member rarely uses, so to increase the value of these existing benefits, associations can offer more flexible or affordable options for accessing the benefit.

Think about your assets that required a significant investment but are used infrequently; you may identify the next wave in peer-to-peer access. Although some traditional organizations such as taxi services and hotel chains have tried to get legislation passed that would restrict or stall disrupters from creating more platforms that enable individuals to share their assets as a way to earn revenue, it is unlikely the concept will disappear. Rather than fight against consumer behavior, trends, and attitudes, organizations need to pivot.

This brings us back to how associations may be able to better leverage the business model being used by consumers and sellers in the new economy. From membership to meeting registration, associations could create a platform that would allow members to provide access to their benefits with colleagues or peers, resulting in a lower per person cost and a higher reach for the organization.

Learning to Share: Bikes, Luxury Cars, Workplaces, and More

When a sharing economy idea gains momentum and users are quick to participate, it is most often because it solves a problem. To illustrate, I've identified different variations of the sharing economy business model. A hybrid model provides the assets, such as bikes, workspaces, or cars, and allows individuals to choose how they wish to use it based on flexible time and payment options. With a collaborative business model, the organization has built a platform that brings together buyers and sellers but does not own any assets. In both models, a mobile app provides an easy and accessible way for individuals to connect. Payments are flexible, and the user determines the frequency of the use. In other words, you don't need to pay for an item or rental space unless you are using it.

Although both business models provide an interesting alternative to the traditional model of ownership, long-term contracts, or paying for benefits you don't frequently use, not every new idea succeeds or is profitable. Sometimes the first company to try an idea fails, but later companies are able to improve upon the original idea or design. The companies profiled below may not be the first to try an idea or may not have long-term success, but they offer a blueprint from which associations can draw valuable insights on leveraging the sharing economy.

Divvy Bike Share

Divvy is a publicly available bike program in Chicago that allows users to easily pay for and unlock a bike and ride it for 30 minutes. Motivate, the corporate parent of Divvy and the largest bike-share operator in North America, helped the City of Chicago launch Divvy by providing an efficient, safe, and affordable program. Calling itself a "vertically integrated company," Motivate also helps design and deploy the technology needed to support bike-sharing programs in cities across the United States.

If you've visited Chicago, Boston, New York City, the Bay Area in California, or Washington, DC, within the last five years, you've likely seen their brightly colored bikes on the road or parked at a station. Similar to other cities, with Divvy in Chicago, it is primarily intended as an alternative way to get around the city quickly and affordably. With 580 stations and 5,800 bikes, it's easy to see why it's a popular choice for transportation. Riders can pay for a single 30-minute trip, a 24-hour pass, or an annual pass. A transit app makes it easy to create an account and unlock a bike, and you can return your bike to any station within the city. Because it saves users time, is convenient, and is good for the environment, many commuters are now using the system year-round to get around

Chicago—even in the cold winter months. In 2017, approximately 37,000 annual members belonged to the Divvy program, and more than 337,000 day passes were sold that year.[12] Divvy plans to integrate its bike-sharing program with the local commuter train Ventra card to make it even easier to pay and use its bikes.[13]

Although the Divvy bike-share program in Chicago experienced a growth in ridership every year since its launch, not every aspect of the program has been a success. In an effort to diversify its ridership and expand opportunities into other neighborhoods, the City of Chicago built Divvy stations in lower income areas. Although the intention was to expand access to underserved populations, the initiative did not prove to be a financial success or hit its ridership targets.[14] The Boston bike-sharing program has had more success expanding to underserved populations, which the National Association of City Transportation Officials partly attributed to the city's outreach efforts and the program having a simple process for joining the discount membership option.[15]

As exemplified by the growing reach of bike-sharing programs, the shift from an ownership-based business model to a shared business model will affect almost every industry. Technology advancements combined with changing attitudes, preferences, and behaviors will drive more consumers toward companies that offer a pay-as-you-go model. Although there may always be a market for expensive, well-made bicycles, programs like the Divvy bike-share program mark the emergence of a trend that is likely to continue for many years.

Two significant forces have been driving the speed of success of bike-sharing programs in the United States over the past five years. For one, the operator, Motivate, targeted cities with a commuter population and an interest in providing a healthy, accessible, and sustainable alternative to residents and visitors. Motivate provided municipalities with a business model that included operational support, marketing and promotion assistance, technology innovations, and sponsorship opportunities. Second, the timing of the bike-sharing programs coincided with a shift in attitudes on consumption habits, with more demand for environmentally friendly solutions, affordable alternatives to mass transportation, and digital access via a mobile phone.

WeWork Shared Office Space

In less than 10 years, WeWork turned an idea for a network of shared office spaces into a network of more than 200 work spaces around the globe, more than 200,000 members,[16] and more than $4 billion in funding.[17] WeWork also boasts 22 percent of Fortune 500 companies as members.[18] The founders of WeWork, Adam Neumann and Miguel McKelvey, originally launched as Green Desk in 2008. They believed individuals wanted a more sustainable or green work environment—recycled furniture, free-trade coffee, and green office supplies. Because the Great Recession came quickly on the heels of launching its first shared work space, many of their first customers, called members, were individuals who had been laid off and were looking to launch a new business. But it wasn't environmental sustainability that attracted members to Green Desk; it was the community. In 2010, Neumann and McKelvey sold their interest in Green Desk, and WeWork was launched in a 3,000-square-foot space in New York City.[19]

What differentiates WeWork from other shared working environments is the shared social experience, or community, that is built into the business model. Beyond the must-have amenities such as high-speed internet connections, package handling, and office furniture, members can take advantage of many free perks, including micro-roasted coffee, fruit water, living-room style lounges, craft beer events, and professional networking and learning programs. From workshops to thought-leader panels and cheese tastings, WeWork can help organizations nurture a stronger team culture. McKelvey told *Business Insider,* "It was always thought of, 'How can we support this person who wants to live more collectively, live lighter—who wants to have less stuff, who wants to pursue their passion, pursue a life of meaning, rather than looking for just material success?'"[20]

In addition to shared work spaces, WeWork offers an alternative to short-term residential leases through its WeLive program. Building upon the success of community wellness and living, WeLive residences include a chef's kitchen, a communal dining room, a fitness center, and regular social events. And while WeWork is based on co-working, the company employs yoga instructors, architects, teachers, molecular biologists, and social psychologists to provide its members with a wellness program to enhance their memberships.[21]

Years before WeWork opened its doors, IWG (also known as Regus) offered shared work spaces in major cities across the globe. What's different about the WeWork business model is that it tapped into a key benefit that was missing from existing models. More than a place to plug in your laptop, the company's mission is to "create a world where people work to make a life, not just a living." WeWork offers its members a physical space that enables collaboration for teams of any size. It offers a community that encourages connections. And it offers tangible services to its members, including healthcare options, payment processing, information technology, education, training and more.[22] Financially, it offers companies, small and large, a way to provide all of the perks of a startup at a lower operational cost.

1871

Designed for entrepreneurs, 1871 was created to support Chicago's digital startup community. Located in the Merchandise Mart in Chicago, the organization is the home of more than 400 early-stage digital startups, as well as the headquarters and satellite offices for more established organizations. Its name is derived from the story of what happened after the Great Chicago Fire of 1871 when the city was rebuilt by engineers, architects, and inventors. Its purpose is to offer a place where organizations can "share ideas, make mistakes, work hard, build their business, and … change the world."[23] It's the physical establishment of what many associations strive to offer their members. Even when their members are healthcare professionals or engineers, financial advisors or librarians, if they wish to succeed in their chosen vocations, they understand the importance of having an ecosystem to support their efforts.

Membership in 1871 offers lifestyle amenities such as treadmill desks, nursing rooms, and laundry services. But what drives companies to apply for membership is the ability to network with potential mentors, investors, board members, corporate partners, and other entrepreneurs. Membership also gives business owners access to events featuring technology leaders, venture capitalists, and other influencers in the community. Members receive unlimited access to more than 30 workshops a month and discounted rates for student loan repayment programs, recruiting services, and media support.

Collaboration is at the center of 1871's business model. Similar to the traditional association model, membership provides access to a unique set of benefits. But it's the sense of inclusiveness and collaboration that is required of all participants that fuels the engine. Unlike traditional associations where members may join but not engage, 1871 works when everyone is engaged.

ReachNow

Referring to its offerings as an "ecosystem of mobility services" on its website, ReachNow is a car-sharing program that lets users drive (or in some areas, ride as a passenger in) one of their more than 1,300 BMWs and MINI vehicles in Seattle; Portland, Oregon; and New York City. With more than 85,000 members as of June 2018, members can pick up a car on the street; drive it for an hour, a day, or longer; and then drop it off anywhere within their designated home area. The goal is to make urban transportation easier, more cost effective, and fun. ReachNow is not the only player in the car-sharing game. Rather than seeing car sharing as a threat to sales, automaker General Motors recently helped launch an on-demand, short-term rental program of GM-owned vehicles called Maven Reserve. Similar to the car sharing service Zipcar, which provides members with access to short-term car rentals through an easy-to-use reservation and unlocking system, the GM-sponsored company offers an option for individuals who wish to participate in the ride share or gig economy but may not have the means or desire to own a car.[24]

Tradesy

Tracy DiNunzio launched Tradesy in 2012 as a way to simplify her life and safely sell the items in her closet she no longer used but believed others would enjoy. Ironically, she initially built the company while sleeping on her couch and renting her bedroom on Airbnb to finance its creation. Her belief in sustainable consumption—and making it as easy to sell used luxury items as it is to buy new ones—became the framework for a company that today serves millions of customers. The company strives to make fashion resale simple, safe, and stylish by bringing together buyers and sellers.

Not quite an overnight success, the company initially ran on a shoe-string budget from a combination of credit card debt, loans, and revenue from DiNunzio's Airbnb rental. Her first company, Recycled Bride, created in 2009, focused on helping couples unload gently used but still valuable wedding items. As peer-to-peer marketplaces were beginning to find a market, she recognized an opportunity to transition Recycled Bride into a larger platform that enables women to monetize their closets. "A sharing economy platform can aggregate massive amounts of inventory more quickly and cheaply than retailers because our inventory is crowd-sourced from users," said DiNunzio in an interview.[25] She added, "With peer-to-peer commerce platforms that remove the friction and risk from multiparty transactions, consumers are being empowered to value and sell their space, their belongings, and their time in ways that weren't previously possible." The idea has changed how DiNunzio views consumer goods. Rather than owning them, she enjoys them for a period of time and assumes they will take on a new life with someone else. She calls it a "reimagined concept of ownership that's focused on utility rather than possession and can ultimately result in consumers enjoying more variety for their dollar."

ClassPass

I've tried it all. Cycling, barre, yoga, Pilates, health clubs, park district clubs, and heart rate-based interval training programs. I haven't tried boxing yet, but it is on my list. I've held annual memberships, six-month memberships, and punch cards. As a road warrior, business owner, mom, and avid runner, it isn't easy to fit a workout into my day, let alone plan ahead and register for a popular class. I love to try new workout programs, and I enjoy the group experience, but I also find that long-term memberships lock me into something that I can't fully use.

It turns out I'm not alone in my quest for a more flexible way to take classes from a variety of studios. After having trouble finding a dance class to take after work in New York City, Payal Kadakia set out to solve the problem of finding and booking an exercise class when and where it is most convenient. And with that idea, ClassPass was created. Its mission is to "motivate people to lead inspired lives every day by introducing and seamlessly connecting them to soul-nurturing experiences." To do this, ClassPass offers a monthly subscription service with access to a network of boutique fitness studios and gyms. When ClassPass first launched, subscribers paid a flat monthly fee of $45 to gain access to five fitness classes a month. The business model changed in 2018 to providing a certain number of class credits for a monthly fee, and studios may set requirements on how many credits must be used to take a class. It also increased its inventory and offers a three-tier subscription program based on location, fees, credits, and number of classes that may be booked each month. For example, for $35 a month, a subscriber can receive 20 credits that may be used to book two to three classes. The ClassPass may be used in any studio partner in one of 50 cities included in the network. The company also launched a stand-alone subscription program for unlimited live and on-demand workouts you can take in your home.

The popularity of ClassPass rests on its ability to provide a flexible, accessible, and digital solution. By focusing on small group classes rather than access to a larger gym, it promotes its ability to provide best-in-class instructors while being supported and motivated by other members of the group. However, the change in the pricing model is leaving some ClassPass members unsure if there is enough value to continue.[26] While flexibility, mobile access, and value are hallmarks of the ClassPass business model, individuals may allow their subscriptions to lapse if they no longer believe they can receive a better deal through the program than if they signed up for a gym membership. Traditional gyms have an opportunity to compete with companies such as ClassPass by creating more flexible options that reinforce the value and adjust to changing circumstances. Many full-service fitness clubs promote the wide array of fitness classes, a mobile app for easy class registrations, and the luxury of a full-service spa and locker room. It's an experience that is different from the boutique or specialty fitness studios that have been sprouting up across the country (think Orangetheory Fitness and SoulCycle).

SpotHero

SpotHero does not own or operate any parking garages. It has no inventory, yet it offers drivers numerous parking options at discounted rates. SpotHero provides an alternative to paying a high daily parking fee or driving around looking for an open parking spot. Instead, users use the mobile app to search, reserve, and pay for a convenient parking space based on location and price. You have complete control over how much you are willing to pay and how long you need the spot. Once you enter your desired location into the app, a variety of parking spaces at different price points are shown. Best of all, the spot will be reserved and waiting for you when you arrive. To enter and exit the parking spot, you can use the app, an email confirmation, or a printed receipt and bar code. Prices are lower because SpotHero finds unused parking spaces and helps fill them for garage operators. If you own a parking spot in a frequently visited area, you may also get your spot listed on SpotHero and rent it to others when you are not using it.

The origins of the sharing economy business model could be traced to a variety of factors that have driven change since the early 2000s. There is a growing interest in sharing unused assets and saving money, and it has touched nearly every aspect of our lives, from hospitality to transportation and from consumer goods to entertainment. Applying the concepts of the sharing or access economy to the association community takes patience, insight into how changing attitudes and behaviors will impact purchasing, and a willingness to risk failure when building a new business model.

It Comes Down to Value: Understanding the Drivers Behind Behavior

What's driving the sharing economy is value—delivered by reducing transaction costs and by helping buyers and sellers find each other in an easy to use, safe, and efficient environment. In 2016, more than 400 venture-financed companies raised more than $23 billion to transform the way individuals interact, collaborate, and buy and sell goods and services.[27] From construction equipment and machinery access to food, flights, and storage programs, the peer-to-peer programs are meeting the needs of consumers who want more flexibility and value when they make a purchase decision.

Motivations

A growing desire for community, convenience, and savings helped push interest and participation in programs that allow individuals to share— rather than own—consumer goods. The sharing economy creates social connections. The Great Recession most likely accelerated the pace at which individuals were willing to try new ideas and trust new companies because there was an urgent need for more affordable work spaces, travel options, dining, and so forth. And while the earliest adopters may have been predominantly classified as millennials, the generation gap began to close as individuals of all ages gained a greater sense of trust and comfort in the services being offered through the shared economy.

Technology enabling transactions and building trust

The ecosystem of the sharing economy rests on the technology platforms that enable individuals to interact with others. It connects supply and demand and enables owners and operators to earn income from underused goods and services. From searching an online marketplace to completing a peer-to-peer transaction, rapid advancements in technology and the use of mobile apps have fueled the growth of the sharing economy. And while some online reviews may not be honest or may be slightly embellished, many sharing economy companies have established guarantees and a rating system to alleviate many concerns. Even as global trust in advertising takes a nosedive, especially in an age of fake news sites and data breaches, individuals appear to place enough trust in their peers to use many of the sharing economy companies mentioned in this book.

At a minimum, organizations that want to build a sharing economy business model must incorporate the following components into their systems:

1. **Search functionality and data analytics.** If you want members, prospects, and customers to turn to your organization first, it must offer a powerful, relevant, and easy to use search tool. Behind the scenes, organizations should be analyzing search terms, downloads,

and purchases to recommend other resources that will be of interest based on certain behaviors.

2. **Reviews and an online community.** Your core membership may understand the unique value you offer and the high quality of work delivered by your organization, but individuals with little to no connection with your organization are more likely to be influenced by peer reviews and recommendations. As you build a sharing economy business model, the technology platform should include a component that allows the community of users to share their experiences and connect with one another. While many organizations offer an online community as a member benefit, by shifting your perspective on the purpose of the community, you may attract larger participation among your primary, secondary, and tertiary audiences.

3. **Mobile access to initiate and complete transactions.** Building a sharing economy business model requires providing access via a mobile app, responsive design, or a website optimized for mobile phones. This holds true for both online and in-person shared benefits. The portability of mobile phones means your benefits should also be portable.

4. **Self-service functionality.** The world does not operate in the traditional 9-to-5 timeframe. Regardless if your members and customers work early, midday, or late shifts, individuals seek and use resources that are available 24/7. If they have questions or concerns, they will need assistance when it is convenient for them, not for you. Organizations must create self-service pathways to help members and customers easily find the answers they need. This may include your online community, easy to use Q&A forums, and automated chatbots using artificial intelligence.

Access over ownership

An Audi A4, a Louis Vuitton handbag, and a private seaside house with views of the ocean—if it were not for the sharing economy, most consumers might never use any of these items. And while it is fun to drive an Audi A4 or vacation in a seaside cottage, the cost of ownership may not be in your budget, but that doesn't diminish the desire to temporarily experience these items. Individuals who participate in the sharing economy often value access to goods and services over ownership. For those who may desire an expensive experience, such as a luxury car or vacation home, the opportunity offered by a sharing economy company will give them instant gratification and a sense of excitement that could have only previously been obtained if they had the means to purchase the item or experience. And borrowing the item for a limited time means removing the costs and hassle of maintenance.

Accelerating the shift from ownership to access may also be the growing income inequality in America, a bifurcated workforce, and industry consolidation. I have observed a trend of employers, including many within industries that are funded by venture capitalists, increasingly hiring only mission-critical employees and expanding the use of part-time employees, freelancers, or contract workers to fill other roles. When this occurs, financial support for membership and continuing education are likely to be offered to full-time employees, whereas part-time or contract workers will need to pay for their own education and dues. And while the data has yet to be collected to support this observation, if you wait until it is available, it is usually too late to respond. While the needs of workers in the gig economy still need to be addressed, the traditional membership or registration model may be unrealistic as they search for alternatives for keeping their skills updated and networking with others.

According to *ASAE ForesightWorks,* the inequality within America has grown since the 1970s, as the share of wealth continues to rise among the top 1 percent.[28] Combine this observation with the increase in student debt, and it's no wonder that many prospective members may be more interested in paying for shared access to benefits that provide a return on their investments than joining an organization.

Thinking back to the examples I've given of items individuals are likely to use but not own, traditional and well-established companies offer many options. You can buy a new car with many of the features offered in an Audi A4 but at a lower price; however, it won't provide the same experience as driving an Audi or allow you to forgo the added expense of insurance, maintenance, and parking. If you travel to another city to attend a conference, visit family, or vacation, Marriott and Hyatt offer a variety of options at different prices and in convenient locations. Yet these options often require travelers to pay a higher fee to access the internet or dine in one of their restaurants. As individuals seek solutions, they will most likely consider the overall experience and cost before making a decision—and the sharing economy may provide a better solution.

Although continuing education and access to information are not luxury items, many individuals and organizations do not have the budgets to pay for more than one membership or attend an in-person conference. Ironically, some conference attendees may use Airbnb and Uber to lower the costs associated with traveling to an event.

Many employers will only pay for continuing education if it helps their professional staff maintain their licenses. Nurses, for example, may pay membership dues out of their own pockets and receive a small stipend to attend a continuing education event. As such, it is unlikely they will join a specialty medical society in addition to paying dues to a specialty nursing organization, even if they are offered a membership at a highly discounted rate. Being able to access a colleague's membership resources may be the best option for a nurse who wishes to obtain members-only information on a sub-specialty healthcare topic.

Frictionless transactions aligning with consumer behavior

Walk into a Starbucks in any city or airport in the United States and you will likely see customers paying for their orders using the Starbucks mobile app. The app allows customers to skip the line by ordering and paying for their food or beverage before they arrive at the store. And while Starbucks may have been one of the early adopters of the technology, many of its competitors now offer a mobile order and pay option. By providing a frictionless transaction, Starbucks is responding to the changing way people want to pay for goods and services. And while retailers and restaurants are beginning to expand into digital payments, it's long been a hallmark of the sharing economy.

A frictionless transaction makes it easy for an individual to make a purchase without pulling out their credit card. When convenience is a driving factor in the purchase decision, making the transaction frictionless can mean the difference between closing the sale and losing a customer.

Today, if you make a purchase on Amazon, the process is frictionless. Once you've selected the items you wish to purchase, you may choose one-click ordering or add it to your cart, and the rest of the transaction is completed with very little effort. Blockchain technology may or may not accelerate the use of digital currency, but it is unlikely that consumers will want to pull out their wallets to pay for goods and services in the future when there is a more efficient way to complete the transaction.

If your association does not offer frictionless transactions, it may be losing customers to alternative solutions, even if their products are inferior in quality. If it is good enough, a frictionless encounter may provide enough value to keep coming back. Your association needs to streamline the process for members interacting with your association. This isn't a technology solution; it's a strategic initiative—to save members and customers time and remove the friction from engaging with your organization.

In a move that reflects the changing nature of security and how trans-actions are made today, the four major credit card networks announced they would no longer need retailers to require a signature when completing a transaction. And while there are some occasions when a signature on a receipt coincides with providing a tip, I suspect alternative options using digital payments or built-in service charges may replace the slower checkout process. Whereas a signature previously provided an added level of security, today it slows down the payment process.

Fairness, regulatory concerns, and competition

What hasn't gone unnoticed by government agencies and traditional companies are the compliance fees and tax revenue many organiza-tions believe should be paid by companies such as Airbnb, Lyft, and others. In addition, the larger the platform, the more difficult it is for new companies to enter the market. As the battle escalates between traditional companies and ones that use a sharing economy business model, it is likely that consumers will experience some changes in fees and acces-sibility. The question that remains is what ultimately drives individuals to become repeat customers. If it is ease of use, accessibility, and control, they are likely to stay with the new model.

Lessons Learned and Action Steps for a Sharing Economy

1. To stay relevant, focus on the key characteristics of a sharing economy business model—access, flexibility, affordability and value, trust, and community—and keep adapting the model as technology advances and needs change. Although each of the models showcased in this book provides an alternative approach to a traditional way of conducting business, they will probably only survive if they continue to evolve as well. From the time this book was written to when it is published, new organizations may be competing with these companies, and behaviors and technology may once again change the landscape.

2. Build upon your strengths. A value proposition that enables your association to be all things to all people is impossible to achieve. Some individuals and organizations may never join your association or attend your multiday conference. Creating a new membership category may stretch your resources too thin and make it nearly impossible to achieve your goals. However, leveraging your strengths and creating new opportunities for prospective customers to engage with your organization may ultimately help you achieve your organization's mission and vision and expand your reach.

3. Embrace change. Needs change. Interests change. Willingness to join and renew will change over time. What your members need at the beginning of their careers differs from their needs as they gain knowledge and experience. In many instances, these needs are likely to drive the decision to become more or less engaged with an organization.

   Many of today's business models were created on an assumption that members would be willing to pay for all of the benefits bundled with membership even when they are no longer needed because they believe it is essential to belong or support the organization's mission or because membership is part of their professional identity. In reality, this isn't the case. To decrease the likelihood of losing members as their needs change, associations need to offer different options for engaging with the organization.

Creating a business model that allows members to share their benefits may help your organization keep at-risk members who are likely to allow their memberships to lapse. It also helps your organization engage with hard-to-reach audiences who may never join but may be interested in your products and services. It may even help your organization create stronger connections with transactional members and customers. Whether their communities include c-suite executives or young professionals, business owners or staff, the healthcare team or caregivers, organizations should consider more flexible options if they wish to provide a reasonable return on the investment of time and money.

4. Monitor and track trends to remain relevant as attitudes and behaviors change. At a minimum, organizations should conduct an environmental scan, frequent online polls, and in-depth surveys with members, lapsed members, and customers. *ASAE ForesightWorks* is one of the most comprehensive, evidence-based research initiatives designed to help associations with environmental scanning and planning for change. The complete collection includes 41 action briefs and the user's guide. Each action set focuses on six to eight drivers of changes in a specific area of interest, including

- content, learning, and knowledge
- data and technology
- demographics and membership
- economic conditions
- society and politics
- workforce and workplace[29]

Other good sources for tracking consumer trends are Trend Hunter and the Pew Research Center. According to Trend Hunter's website, more than 200,000 contributors provide ideas and insights to help it drive innovation with some of the world's largest brands. The Pew Research Center is a nonpartisan fact tank that informs the public about issues, attitudes, and trends shaping the world. It conducts public opinion polling, demographic research, content analysis, and other data-driven social science research. Research areas include U.S. politics and policy, journalism and media, internet and technology, science and society, religion and public life, Hispanic trends, global attitudes and trends, and social and demographic trends.

5. Before designing a business model that embraces the sharing economy, establish short-term and long-term goals and align them with the organization's strategic plan. Many organizations are beginning to define success as expanding their reach rather than their membership base. To expand your reach, you may need to rethink the value of a customer. If your mission and vision include a focus on enhancing the profession or advancing a cause, membership may not be the number one priority for your association. If your membership campaigns have not yielded the results in increasing your market share, consider implementing a business model that will help you expand your reach by allowing individuals to share their membership benefits.

6. Capitalize on the sharing economy and engage new audiences by building a new business model for a program, product, service, or membership.

   a. Begin by identifying a list of audience segments who should be using your products and services but have not joined the organization. The list may include professionals within your primary audience as well as those who work with them but in a different capacity.

   b. Identify a list of benefits that you believe are most likely being shared by members. If you are unsure, conduct a survey to understand how members use and pass along information to others. The study can help identify what is currently being shared, with whom, and when.

   c. Create an add-on program that allows current members to add-on additional "household members" to their accounts. Once you've identified the list of products and services you are willing to allow members to share, you can develop different financial models with break even and growth scenarios. This will help your organization determine a price and the size of the market that is needed to achieve your goals.

7. To minimize risk, create a feedback loop and conduct market testing with key audiences. Identify a group of participants who meet the criteria you've established for your target audience. Make it easy for them to provide feedback and respond quickly to their questions. Be prepared to make changes to the program because few successful business models look exactly as they were originally designed, and few business models remain unchanged from the initial idea through full implementation.

•

Qualities of Association Leaders

One thing that struck me while interviewing association c-suite executives was how many of them act like entrepreneurs. For one, they embrace change: changes in the market; changes in the culture; changes in the way programs, products, and services are developed and delivered. They understand it is part of running an organization and being nimble. They believe change leads to positive outcomes, even when they encounter obstacles or have some failures along the way.

As a related quality, they recognize the importance of risk-taking. They embrace an idea I've heard shared by other entrepreneurs: You shouldn't bet the company, but every once in a while, you should bet your job. They believe it is important to understand how failure is a part of success. This isn't just a statement. They didn't just take risks by investing in new products or programs but also in new methodologies, new technology, and new organizational structures. They invest in new ideas and are willing to risk failure and learn from it. For these executives, this means investing money, time, and resources in something they didn't know would work. In some cases, it did. In others, it didn't. For the latter, they followed the mantra of "fail fast and learn."

Many of them also set big goals. This may seem like an obvious one, but it's a characteristic that often falls in the "said, but not done" category. These leaders said, Double our revenue. Double our membership. Broaden our reach. Launch a new society. Significantly increase our relevance and influence on political issues.

Some of the other similarities are

- **A desire to learn from others.** They have a desire to expand their knowledge. They are confident—not that they have all of the answers but that they can find the answers. And they never stop searching for ways to improve or expand what they know.

- **A proactive rather than reactive approach.** They have an abundance mindset rather than a scarcity or fixed mentality. They see a wealth of resources and opportunities rather than limits on what can be accomplished.

- **A focus on the value proposition.** They understand that without value, it is difficult to build a sustainable membership organization. Understanding what the organization can offer and what it is uniquely positioned to provide is essential to providing value. This also means knowing their members, the profession, and the industry better than anyone—in other words, knowing more than the members themselves about the needs of the community. Research and data analytics play a major role in this.

- **A belief in the importance of trust, transparency, and clarity of purpose.** They ask and seek answers to important but difficult questions. Why do we exist, what do we want to accomplish, and how will we get there? As they search for the answers, they are transparent in their approaches, and they establish a level of trust with their boards and staff.

These leaders also emphasized the need to get the right people in the room, whether on staff, as consultants, or on the board. As Susan Neely from the American Beverage Association said, you need to "get the whole brain together" when implementing major changes.

- **Get the right people on the team to support the goals.** In some cases, this means a lean management team and the use of consultants and experts. Others mix it up by hiring a combination of association executives and individuals from outside the association community (e.g., industry and non-industry experts). Nearly all of the executives interviewed made changes to their senior management teams.

- **Get the right folks on the board.** First, it's important to ask, do the board members reflect the community, and can they speak to the interests of different members within the community? Second, will they have the oversight, insight, foresight, and hindsight needed to guide the organization forward? Third, will they accept change? Are they willing to accept failure under their watch if it means the organization will ultimately learn something and move forward?

Many of the executives did not come into a turnaround situation. The organizations were functioning fine but had experienced little or no growth in terms of revenue or reach in recent times. Some were seeing a slow decline in membership, but it didn't warrant a complete turnaround. Sometimes, these situations can be even more difficult for association leaders—it's harder to get buy-in from the board and staff of a risk-averse organization when they can't foresee an imminent crisis. But a lesson many organizations have had to learn in times of rapid change is you need to adapt to environmental changes because the environment won't adapt to you.

As part of their pivots, a few organizations recognized that membership growth is not always the solution. Organizations like the Medical Group Management Association and Entomological Society of America focused on maintaining their memberships and growing their customer base or reach instead. A few organizations narrowed their focus to what they could uniquely and exclusively do well. Organizations like the Ohio Society of Certified Public Accountants and the National Restaurant Association don't offer hundreds of different product lines; they instead create product extensions in areas that are relevant to their missions and provide value to the community. Many are also dedicated to collecting and sharing industry research and publish regular state of the industry reports (e.g., National Restaurant Association, Society of Gynecologic Oncology, American Beverage Association). By doing so, they not only share important and relevant information, but they also are able to forecast issues, challenges, and opportunities on the horizon and respond with solutions.

CONCLUSION

•

The Pivot Readiness Checklist

Using the five essential characteristics described in Chapter 2, the checklist below will enable your association to evaluate its readiness to pivot to adapt to a changing environment and to meet shifting needs and behaviors.

For each question, indicate whether your association

- Is fully optimized
- Has started the process, but more needs to be done
- Has begun to discuss it/plan for it
- Hasn't considered it at all

Key Tenet: **Access(ibility)**	Yes, we are fully optimized	To some degree but more needs to be done	We have begun to discuss it/ plan for it	No
Has your organization prioritized digital accessibility of most of your organization's primary benefits?				
Is your organization's technology infrastructure nimble enough to adapt to changing behaviors and usages of digital technology?				

Key Tenet: **Flexibility**	Yes, we are fully optimized	To some degree but more needs to be done	We have begun to discuss it/ plan for it	No
Do members and customers have multiple options (e.g., mobile app, journals, webinars, in-person events) for accessing the majority of information and content you offer?				
Do members have multiple options for volunteering or engaging with your association (ad hoc to more in-depth)?				
Do members have multiple options to join your organization at different price points?				

Key Tenet: **Affordability**	Yes, we are fully optimized	To some degree but more needs to be done	We have begun to discuss it/ plan for it	No
Are your programs, products, and services priced to accommodate different audiences across income and experience levels (e.g., students, recent graduates, unemployed)?				

Key Tenet: **Diversity & Inclusion**	Yes, we are fully optimized	To some degree but more needs to be done	We have begun to discuss it/ plan for it	No
Does your board of directors represent a range of ages and experience levels?				
Do your board of directors and staff represent a diversity of thought and perspective?				

Key Tenet: **Diversity & Inclusion**	Yes, we are fully optimized	To some degree but more needs to be done	We have begun to discuss it/ plan for it	No
Does your board of directors include a range of subspecialties or interest areas in the profession?				
Does your board of directors represent the profession in terms of workplace setting and geographical locations?				
Does your association have a policy on what behavior will not be tolerated at events or in the workplace?				
Does your organization examine its policies and procedures to ensure it creates a welcoming environment for all members and staff?				

Key Tenet: **Trust**	Yes, we are fully optimized	To some degree but more needs to be done	We have begun to discuss it/ plan for it	No
Is there a high level of trust among staff across different departments?				
Is there a high level of trust among volunteer leaders?				
Do association staff trust the volunteer leaders to make decisions that are good for the association overall?				
Do volunteer leaders trust the staff to act on the board's strategic direction?				

Endnotes

Chapter 1: A Changing Landscape

1. Scott D. Anthony and others, "2018 Corporate Longevity Forecast: Creative Destruction is Accelerating," Innosight, www.innosight.com/insight/creative-destruction/.

2. Ilan Mochari, "Why Half of the S&P 500 Companies Will Be Replaced in the Next Decade," *Inc.*, March 23, 2016, www.inc.com/ilan-mochari/innosight-sp-500-new-companies.html.

3. Clayton M. Christensen, Michael E. Raynor, and Rory MacDonald, "What is Disruptive Innovation?", *Harvard Business Review,* December 2015, https://hbr.org/2015/12/what-is-disruptive-innovation.

4. Christensen Institute, "Jobs to Be Done," www.christenseninstitute.org/jobs-to-be-done/.

5. Chris Isidore, "Amazon didn't kill Toys 'R' Us. Here's what did," CNN Money, March 15, 2018, http://money.cnn.com/2018/03/15/news/companies/toys-r-us-closing-blame/index.html.

6. Todd Leopold, "The death and life of a great American bookstore," CNN, September 12, 2011, www.cnn.com/2011/US/09/12/first.borders.bookstore.closing/index.html.

Chapter 2: Five Essential Characteristics

1. Charles Moore, "Chapter XXV: Closing In. 1911-1912," *Daniel H. Burnham, Architect, Planner of Cities Volume 2* (Boston and New York: Houghton Mifflin Company, 1921), 147. Also available online at http://archive.org/stream/danielhburnhamar02moor#page/147/mode/1up.

2. Joshua Topolsky, "I used Google Glass: the future, but with monthly updates," *The Verge,* February 22, 2013, www.theverge.com/2013/2/22/4013406/i-used-google-glass-its-the-future-with-monthly-updates.

3. Nick Bilton, "Why Google Glass Broke," *The New York Times*, February 4, 2015, www.nytimes.com/2015/02/05/style/why-google-glass-broke.html.

4. Marsha L. Rhea, CAE, *ASAE ForesightWorks User's Guide: Designing Your Association's Journey Into Foresight* (Washington, DC: ASAE: The Center for Association Leadership, 2018), 10.

5. *Ibid.*, 4.

6. Michael Miller, *Online Marketing Heroes: Interviews with 25 Successful Online Marketing Gurus* (Indianapolis: Wiley Publishing, Inc., 2008), 68.

7. Robert Reiss, "Tony Hsieh on His Secrets of Success," *Forbes*, July 1, 2010, www.forbes.com/2010/07/01/tony-hsieh-zappos-leadership-managing-interview.html#665128656d4e.

8. Retail TouchPoints, "55% Of Consumers Welcome Customer Service Chatbots," November 17, 2017, www.retailtouchpoints.com/features/news-briefs/55-of-consumers-welcome-customer-service-chatbots.

9. Paul Demery, "Why an Omnichannel Strategy Matters," *Digital Commerce 360*, December 31, 2013, www.digitalcommerce360.com/2013/12/31/why-omnichannel-strategy-matters/.

10. Mochari, "Why Half of the S&P 500 Companies Will Be Replaced in the Next Decade," *Inc.*

11. Rhea, *ASAE ForesightWorks User's Guide*.

12. Stephen R. Covey with Rebecca R. Merrill, *The Speed of Trust: The One Thing that Changes Everything* (New York: Free Press, 2008), 40.

13. Christie Smith and Stephanie Turner, "The Radical Transformation of Diversity and Inclusion: The Millennial Influence" (Deloitte Development LLC, 2015), 7. Also available online at www2.deloitte.com/content/dam/Deloitte/us/Documents/about-deloitte/us-inclus-millennial-influence-120215.pdf.

14. *Ibid.*, 8.

Chapter 3: Culture

1. Clayton Christensen, "Disruptive Innovation," www.claytonchristensen.com/key-concepts/.

2. Reed Hastings, "Culture," *SlideShare*, August 1, 2009, https://www.slideshare.net/reed2001/culture-1798664.

3. Nancy Hass, "And the Award for the Next HBO Goes to...," *GQ*, January 29, 2013, https://www.gq.com/story/netflix-founder-reed-hastings-house-of-cards-arrested-development?mobify=0.

4. Bill Taylor, "How Coca-Cola, Netflix, and Amazon Learn from Failure," *Harvard Business Review,* November 10, 2017, https://hbr.org/2017/11/how-coca-cola-netflix-and-amazon-learn-from-failure.

5. Jamie Notter, *Culture That Works: How Getting Serious About Culture Unlocks New Performance* (E-book, 2017), 9.

6. *Ibid.,* 8.

7. *Ibid.,* 4.

8. Rhea, *ASAE ForesightWorks User's Guide.*

9. Carlos Serrao, "The Man Is a Brand," *Men's Health,* December 18, 2003, www.menshealth.com/trending-news/a19526916/the-virgin-groups-richard-branson/.

10. Alex Kacik, "For the first time ever, less than half of physicians are independent," *Modern Healthcare,* May 31, 2017, www.modernhealthcare.com/article/20170531/NEWS/170539971.

11. *Ibid.*

12. Michael Shick, "Jeff Bezos—'What's dangerous is not to evolve,'" *Fast Company,* March 3, 2010, www.fastcompany.com/1569357/jeff-bezos-whats-dangerous-not-evolve.

13. AuthorEarnings, "February 2017 Big, Bad, Wide & International Report: covering Amazon, Apple, B&N, and Kobo ebook sales in the US, UK, Canada, Australia, and New Zealand," http://authorearnings.com/report/february-2017/.

Chapter 4: To Innovate, You Need Value

1. Mark W. Johnson, *Seizing the White Space: Business Model Innovation for Growth and Renewal* (Boston: Harvard Business Press, 2010).

2. Virgin Group, "About Us," www.virgin.com/virgingroup/content/about-us.

3. Virgin Group, "Our Senior Team," www.virgin.com/virgingroup/content/our-senior-team.

4. Virgin Group, "Richard Branson's secrets for success," www.virgin.com/entrepreneur/richard-bransons-secrets-success.

5. Richard Branson, "My top 10 quotes on failure," Virgin Group, www.virgin.com/richard-branson/my-top-10-quotes-failure.

6. Catch Des Moines, "Greater Des Moines Meeting Planner Toolkit," www.catchdesmoines.com/planners/planner-toolkit/.

7. Atlanta Convention & Visitors Bureau, www.atlanta.net.

8. Clayton M. Christensen and Michael E. Raynor, *The Innovator's Solution: Creating and Sustaining Successful Growth* (Boston: Harvard Business School Press, 2003), 99 (footnote 17).

Chapter 5: Become a Five-Star Organization Through Research

1. U.S. Government Accountability Office, *School Meal Programs: Competitive Foods Are Widely Available and Generate Substantial Revenues for Schools*, report to Congressional requestors, August 2005, 15, https://www.gao.gov/new.items/d05563.pdf.

2. Melanie Warner, "Lines Are Drawn for BigSuit Over Sodas," *The New York Times*, December 7, 2005, www.nytimes.com/2005/12/07/business/lines-are-drawn-for-bigsuit-over-sodas.html.

3. Robert F. Wescott, Brendan M. Fitzpatrick, and Elizabeth Phillips, "Industry Self-Regulation to Improve Student Health: Quantifying Changes in Beverage Shipments to Schools," *American Journal of Public Health*, September 12, 2012, https://ajph.aphapublications.org/doi/abs/10.2105/AJPH.2011.300610?prevSearch=wescott&searchHistoryKey=.

4. Christensen, Raynor, and MacDonald, "What is Disruptive Innovation?".

5. Robert E. Gunther, *The Truth About Making Smart Decisions* (FT Press, 2008), 99.

Chapter 6: The Sharing Economy

1. Airbnb, "Fast Facts," https://press.atairbnb.com/fast-facts/.

2. Riley McDermid, "Airbnb's number of listings surpasses rooms held by top 5 hotel brands combined," *San Francisco Business Times*, August 11, 2017, www.bizjournals.com/sanfrancisco/news/2017/08/11/airbnb-surpasses-ihg-wyn-hilton-marriott-listings.html.

3. Airbnb, "About Us," https://press.atairbnb.com/about-us/.

4. Airbnb, "Sharing More About the Technology That Powers Airbnb," March 23, 2018, https://press.atairbnb.com/sharing-more-about-the-technology-that-powers-airbnb/.

5. Neil Irwin, "NBER: U.S. in Recession That Began Last December," *The Washington Post*, December 1, 2008, www.washingtonpost.com/wp-dyn/content/article/2008/12/01/AR2008120101365.html?noredirect=on.

6. Kimberly Amadeo, "The Great Recession of 2008 Explained with Dates," *The Balance*, April 27, 2018, www.thebalance.com/the-great-recession-of-2008-explanation-with-dates-4056832.

7. U.S. Department of Labor, Bureau of Labor Statistics, "The Recession of 2007-2009," February 2012, www.bls.gov/spotlight/2012/recession/.

8. Alan Murray, "The Rise and Rise of Airbnb," *Fortune*, February 15, 2017, http://fortune.com/2017/02/15/airbnb-gallagher-book-inequality-jobs/.

9. Airbnb Blog, "Belong Anywhere," https://blog.atairbnb.com/belong-anywhere/.

10. David Z. Morris, "Today's Cars Are Parked 95% of the Time," *Fortune*, March 13, 2016, http://fortune.com/2016/03/13/cars-parked-95-percent-of-time/.

11. Knowledge@Wharton, "Demographic Shifts: Shaping the Future of Car Ownership," The Wharton School of the University of Pennsylvania, February 21, 2017, http://knowledge.wharton.upenn.edu/article/demographic-shifts-shaping-future-car-ownership/.

12. Sara Freund, "Divvy bikers took a record number of trips in 2017," *Curbed Chicago*, January 5, 2018, https://chicago.curbed.com/2018/1/5/16851818/divvy-bikes-record-number-trips-2017.

13. Fran Spielman, "City working on Ventra-Divvy integration," *The Chicago Sun-Times*, August 14, 2017, https://chicago.suntimes.com/chicago-news/city-working-on-ventra-divvy-integration/.

14. Mary Wisniewski and Gregory Pratt, "Chicago sees drop in Divvy income following expansion into South, West sides," *Chicago Tribune*, December 27, 2017, www.chicagotribune.com/news/local/breaking/ct-met-divvy-income-drop-20171226-story.html.

15. National Association of City Transportation Officials, "Can Monthly Passes Improve Bike Share Equity?", NACTO Bike Share Equity Practitioners' Paper #2, September 2015, https://nacto.org/wp-content/uploads/2015/09/NACTO_Can-Monthly-Passes-Improve-Bike-Share-Equity.pdf.pdf.

16. WeWork Team, "WeWork Celebrates 8th Birthday By Doubling Membership and Revenue," WeWork Blog, February 26, 2018, www.wework.com/blog/posts/wework-celebrates-8th-birthday.

17. Alex Konrad, "WeWork Confirms Massive $4.4 Billion Investment From SoftBank And Its Vision Fund," *Forbes*, August 24, 2017, www.forbes.com/sites/alexkonrad/2017/08/24/wework-confirms-massive-4-4-billion-investment-from-softbank-and-its-vision-fund/#a3f41695b3c4.

18. WeWork Team, "2018 WeWork Economic Impact Report," WeWork Blog, May 8, 2018, www.wework.com/blog/posts/2018-wework-economic-impact-report.

19. Alex Konrad, "Inside the Phenomenal Rise of WeWork," *Forbes*, November 5, 2014, www.forbes.com/sites/alexkonrad/2014/11/05/the-rise-of-wework/#761acbbb6f8b.

20. Melia Robinson, "WeWork, the $17 billion company that simulates startup life, is getting into the fitness business," *Business Insider*, May 25, 2017, www.businessinsider.com/wework-enters-fitness-business-with-wework-wellness-2017-5.

21. David Gelles, "The WeWork Manifesto: First, Office Space. Next, the World," *The New York Times*, February 17, 2018, www.nytimes.com/2018/02/17/business/the-wework-manifesto-first-office-space-next-the-world.html.

22. Bloomberg, "Company Overview of WeWork Companies Inc.," www.bloomberg.com/research/stocks/private/snapshot.asp?privcapId=133839089.

23. 1871, "About 1871," https://1871.com/about/.

24. Kirsten Korosec, "GM's Car-Sharing Service Is Now Offering Monthly Rentals," *Fortune*, March 3, 2017, http://fortune.com/2017/03/03/gm-maven-monthly-service/.

25. Thomas L. Friedman, "How to Monetize Your Closet," *The New York Times*, December 21, 2013, www.nytimes.com/2013/12/22/opinion/sunday/friedman-how-to-monetize-your-closet.html.

26. Zoe Bernard, "ClassPass is tweaking its subscription system and some subscribers aren't happy," *Business Insider*, April 6, 2018, www.businessinsider.com/classpass-credit-price-changes-users-unhappy-2018-4.

27. Judith Wallenstein and Urvesh Shelat, "What's Next for the Sharing Economy?" BCG Henderson Institute, October 4, 2017, www.bcg.com/publications/2017/strategy-technology-digital-whats-next-for-sharing-economy.aspx.

28. Rhea, *ASAE ForesightWorks User's Guide.*

29. *Ibid.*

About the Author

Sheri Jacobs, FASAE, CAE, is a nationally recognized association thought leader, business executive, and author who has spent much of her career helping associations better understand and respond to a rapidly changing environment through research, business modeling, strategic planning, and consulting.

As president and CEO of Avenue M Group, Sheri has helped more than 100 associations, small and large, tackle their most challenging issues. Prior to opening Avenue M Group, Sheri served in staff leadership roles at the American Academy of Implant Dentistry, American Bar Association, and Association Forum of Chicagoland. During her tenure at Association Forum, she built award-winning campaigns that resulted in double-digit membership and meeting attendance growth.

Over the years, Sheri has served in numerous leadership, speaking, and volunteer roles, including chair of the ASAE Membership Council and the ASAE Foundation Development Committee. In 2018, she was selected to serve as a member of the ASAE and the ASAE Foundation Board of Directors. She is author of *The Art of Membership,* co-editor and a contributor to Membership Essentials and author of the ASAE marketing book *199 Ideas: Powerful Marketing Tactics That Sell.*

She is the recipient of numerous awards including the John C. Thiel Distinguished Service Award and the ASAE Academy of Leaders Award. She currently lives in the Chicago Metropolitan area with her daughter and two dogs.

Index